T0129237

The Booklet of "Musings"

. . . and other commentaries, theories, philosophical and social observations, questions and opinions

Bruce Westcott

Order this book online at www.trafford.com
or email orders@trafford.com

Most Trafford titles are also available at major online book retailers.

Printed in the United States of America.

ISBN: 978-1-4669-6446-4 (sc)
ISBN: 978-1-4669-6445-7 (e)

Trafford rev. 10/15/2012

 www.trafford.com

North America & international
toll-free: 1 888 232 4444 (USA & Canada)
phone: 250 383 6864 ♦ fax: 812 355 4082

About the author:

Bruce Westcott has lived through at least two entirely different, extremely diverse and exciting lives . . . and counting.

As an accomplished pianist/singer, Bruce Westcott has entertained international audiences, including at Caesars Palace and The Bellagio Hotel/Casino in Las Vegas for generations.

Bruce performed often for many years at Jilly's in New York City and Palm Springs, California; the Harbor Lounge/Place For Steak on the 79th Street Causeway in Miami Beach; Billy's Elegant Super Club in Washington, D. C.; and the Pimlico Hotel in Baltimore.

Frank Sinatra, for whom Bruce and his trio played many of Mr. Sinatra's private house parties, said that he was one of Bruce's biggest fans. One late night in New York, while Bruce and Frank Sinatra sat alone in a back booth at Jilly's smoking Frank's Lucky Strike cigarettes, Bruce smilingly corrected Frank by saying, "No, Frank; you <u>are</u> my biggest fan."

Following a highly successful career as an entertainer and afterwards as a casino entertainment executive and business entrepreneur, Bruce Westcott entered politics. He did relatively and surprisingly well as a 1998 and 2002 Republican gubernatorial candidate in Nevada

Mr. Westcott then became Chairman of the Reform Party of Nevada and went on to become the National Chairman of a majority faction of the RPUSA, the political party of presidential candidates, Ross Perot, Pat Buchanan and Ralph Nader.

Bruce has received several national and state honors, including being appointed a Kentucky Colonel and was a two-term Committing Magistrate in Maryland.

World-renowned Smithsonian Institute has included a photo of the Caesars Palace marquee featuring, for posterity, Bruce Westcott in one of its special exhibits.

The Pimlico Racetrack, one of three national hosts of the Triple Crown of thoroughbred horse racing, has featured "The Bruce Westcott" as part of the Maryland Jockey Club's centennial celebration.

At the time of this writing, 2011-2012, Bruce Westcott serves as Vice-Chairman of the Reform Party of Nevada, a platform from which he has proffered his political thesis, "Sensible Ideas and Solutions' Formula for America".

From the author:

I would like to remind my readers that in the early 1920's prior to the Great American Wall St. crash, Al Capone had declared the stock market, "A racket".

"It is your work in life that is the ultimate seduction"
—Pablo Picasso

"When the going gets tough, the tough get going."
—Unknown author

"If you can keep your head when all about you are losing
theirs and blaming it on you;
If you can trust yourself when all men doubt you,
But make allowance for their doubting too;
If you can think and not make thoughts your aim,
If you can dream and not make dreams your master;
If you can meet with Triumph and Disaster,
And treat those imposters just the same."—Kipling

"Wet birds never fly at night"—Deadpan comedian, Jackie Vernon

"I never had sex with that woman"—A former President of the United States

Paraphrased: "He who knows, and knows that he knows, ye shall follow."

"You are never given a dream without being given the power to make it come true. You may have to work for it, however."—Unknown author

"Those who don't give up succeed." Taken from a newspaper clipping that has been prominently pasted on my desk for 40 years.

"The truth has a certain ring to it."—Earnest Hemingway

"Do YOU Want The Truth?"—Bruce Westcott

This book is dedicated to my dearly departed brothers, Dickie and Alan, and to my mother, Dorothy Valworth Westcott, who raised all three of us boys and including solely supporting my dear grandmother by working as a "barmaid".

We lived in poverty, but we never knew it.

My mother proudly proclaimed that she "never took a dime from welfare". That alone fills me with pride and admiration for what is all too commonly and pervasively written-off today as a "single mom".

"Musings—and other observations", by Bruce Westcott, who, in expressing his thoughts and opinions, is solely responsible for the following contents:

Every single one of us on Earth is a survivor.

Regardless of what they did or how they did it, every one of us is survived by untold billions of our ancestral survivors.

&

If it's all in the theory of yin and yang, what is on the other side of gravity?

&

Why is it that black people have white soles on their feet and (meant as a compliment) black soul in their hearts?

&

There were "unidentified remains" found in the vicinity of Shanksville, Pennsylvania from the infamous wreckage of Flight #92 on 9-11-2001?

??????

&

A reminder to those of us who have lost friends and family members: We do not completely lose our treasured friends and loved ones to death. They may not be here physically, but they definitely linger with us within the spiritual realm of our thoughts. (And, as some believe, they are possibly waiting for us to join them.)

In life, we enter into, and therefore eternally share each other's cycle of life forever. Which brings up the question of what is and by what measurement constitutes forever?

&

I've struggled with my relationship with God. And with the concept and reality of God. And which God? You know what I mean?

We've all heard the drill: Who or what is God? Why is there God? Where did God come from and who or what created God? Does God actually exist? How do scientists reconcile God vis a vis science, technology and even valid conjecture and theory?

I think that until my entrance into the realm of death provides me with an answer—any answer will suffice to satisfy my curiosity—the concept of God comes down to personal belief. The numerous questions regarding God have either perplexed or, in many cases, solved the forever lingering mystery of the existence of a God—any God according to one's belief. It has always been that way.

Frankly and admittedly, I do have difficulty in believing that God has ever "spoken" directly and specifically to any one human being.

In prayer, we speak to God. I try to speak to God. I certainly believe in the power of God and the spiritual power of prayer to God. I believe that God has heard, or has somehow been conveyed and has therefore selectively accepted at least some of our pleading prayers. But obviously not all. In that context, I believe that God *has* granted certain individuals with certain exceptions through our prayers. We call those exceptions miracles. But mostly, I do have great difficulty in understanding God's ways.

Some people say that God has long-since moved on since The Creation and simply has neither time nor inclination to answer our simple prayerful requests. We're on our own, they say. I tend to believe that assertion.

Unless, of course, God has left behind the spiritual world to assist us.

Why not? Did not God think of everything?

What do you think?

&

One final word regarding God: Does God have a gender? If so, I would think that God is more probably a She.

&

God tests those She loves most.

&

You know, when people so often stumble and pause themselves in conversation with, "you know", don't you want to reply, "No, I don't know" to them?

You know?

&

The Global Economy/The New World Order has proved to be a conceptual economic failure.

However, as I wrote in 1993, I see the world's economic alignment ultimately divided into regional-based, therefore separate, yet globally intertwined economies.

In such a scenario, I predict that most, if not all, national currencies will return to and then remain nationalistically independent. A nation's currency is intrinsically related to a nation's pride, which is the overlooked component of this particular observation that had *not* been considered by world economists when attempting to craft a workable world economic formula.

&

There will always be an Upper Market.

And they will always have protections to insure it.

There will always be a lower-class.

And in my opinion and for the time being, there will be government programs that sustain the poverty levels.

And for decades, the above is the economic model that squeezed the two ends and thereby created the American Middle-Class.

I favor the following paraphrase: At most, give a man or woman a fishing pole and teach them to fish. And personal sharing is both admirable and fine with me, but please do not force it upon me.

America is now in the throes of a social/economic divisive expansion by sustaining the lower-class through government social programs and promoting class warfare, while paradoxically derisively benefiting the rich. As we have seen, this cuts out the middle-class.

However, economically progressive countries around the world have emulated the American model of decades ago that has thusly expanded their middle class by incentivizing their lower class. This, in turn, raises the level and amount of the upper-class.

All boats rise during such an economic tide.

(Thanks, but no thanks to your version of "Change", Mr. Obama.)

Two things:

1) America is merely within a few percentage points of becoming predominantly lower class (why not? where or what is the incentive for working?), and 2) such a change ensures that the economic slavery over the majority keeps the government in power.

&

Moneyacracy:

Definitively, a democratic form of government is designed to govern and legislate by committee. The United States is framed by branches of government that themselves are beholden to committees.

Some will point out that our nation has moved forward quite well as a democracy. France's deTocqueville thought so. However, I'd like to point out that deTocqueville's and others' observations and conclusions were formulated during times of American national unity. Those were times in America's history when political representation was grounded by national causes.

Today, America—and the world—is ruled exclusively by the autocracy of money.

Moneyacracy.

&

A conceivable prediction for your consideration and discussion:

Michele Obama will be American's first woman President of the United States.

At the very least, in 2016 Mrs. Obama will be the Democratic Party's first woman presidential nominee.

The Clinton Era is over.

&

It isn't paranoia if they really are out to get you. You know?

&

Have you thought of how, or by what method or degree of illness or pestilence you will die?

You will die you know.

But how and exactly when?

A very well-to-do friend of mine offered me one million dollars if I could tell him the exact moment in time that I fell asleep the previous night. Or for that matter, any other night.

So, in the same context, and unless we are knowingly scheduled to be executed at a pre-arranged specific time or kill ourselves, how can we possibly ever correctly predict the exact moment, day, week, month or year of our own death?

Think about it . . .

&

"How are you?"

Don't you just love people who ask you that question and then either completely ignore your answer or allow you even a second to respond to the question?

&

"Whatever" is a somewhat disgusting word isn't it when voiced in resignation.

&

Does anyone know how old Mary was when impregnated by the Immaculate Conception?

&

Jesus Christ:

I intend no heresy with the following:

I just wonder if Jesus fathered.

It would seem to me inconceivable in consideration of the period of time and its accepted social circumstances that Jesus would have gone through a young human life sans having any romantic or love interest. (There has been, as you know, some degree or hint of speculation on this subject. See Mary Magdalene.)

I believe that Jesus is the Son of God. But He was also here in the form of a human being, was he not?

Wasn't He thusly then subjected to human emotions?

If you tell me that Jesus was celibate, please prove it, because as far as I know we know virtually nothing about Jesus during his infancy, adolescence, teen and young adult life.

Discuss . . .

&

Regarding, as Freud supposedly coined, The Complex Simple:

Far too much time for entire masses of people is devoted to an after-life rather than the here-and-now life and times.

To my way of thinking, for one to follow that mantra is to waste one's blessing of the gift of life.

&

Can you imagine what it must have been like to have lived in a time during which one of the most important things in life was not your mortgage or a utility bill, but instead of having to avoid having your flesh torn away while you were being eaten by wild animals.

And how about those poor souls who were thrown into the "games" at the Roman Coliseum?

And speaking of burying bodies to neck level . . .

How about the insane torture of burying a person's body, then coating the exposed head with honey and placing the head on an ant pathway?

What other species on Earth, other than cats with mice, torture their victims so furiously?

We claim that we're civilized?

&

Girls, you never really know what you're getting in a man, right?

And men, you never know what you're getting in a woman, right?

Suggestion for guys: If you are getting serious with your girlfriend, I highly recommend that you first check out her mother.

&

I find it interesting that Japan has achieved practically all of its pre-WWII military objectives, not militarily, but rather through economics.

Proving that economics rule and that warring among nations is rather senseless.

&

I have no doubt that the American southern accent is purely derived from English-illiterate Europeans and African slaves.

Test it: Put a black man or woman in a room with a southern white man or woman and then listen only to the tone of the conversation. That's right, except for the grammar, there is no discernible distinction. They all sound the same.

They may not all look the same, but they sure do sound the same.

BTW: Do you know what a cubert is? You would if you're a Southerner.

A cubert is a storage unit that usually contains shelves much similar to a cupboard.

Cubert. ;>)

&

When I went to school there were few fat kids. Nowadays, the word "obese", especially relative to many of today's kids, is practically commonplace.

And today, it seems that the "average American" is definitely overweight.

Don't tell me that there isn't some "unknown ingredient" either in today's food and water or in our modern genetically-engineered food products. I also note that during my school years, there were only a few varieties of soda drinks available. Just saying . . .

(Boy o' boy, that Royal Crown Cola was some nasty stuff.)

Are we drugged into thinking that today's foods and drinks are healthy? Ah, the power of that great deception, Public Relations.

And in the context of this observation, I suggest that soda-warrior, Michael Bloomberg, take a page from Levittown and create Bloomberg.

Then he could completely rule over his domain autocratically and sans opposition. Something to think about Mr. Bloomberg . . . you could name your main thoroughfares Coca Cola Drive, 7-Up Avenue, Dr. Pepper Boulevard . . . just for the Hell of it. Who is going to protest?

&

Have you noticed that it is mostly friends and family who rip you off?

And don't you just love some of the "oh well" responses to your collection efforts?

And wouldn't you just rather kick their asses?

You have to understand that it is basically natural for humans to take from others . . . if you let them.

&

Some people keep a balance sheet on friendships with others. Their rational is stacked up on a, "I did this for you; you did (or did not) this for me" comparative column basis.

Don't you just hate that?

I do know that our nation's foreign policies are based on a balance sheet model. As long as we continue to send (American taxpayers') money, many foreign nations will continue to feint a friendship relationship with America.

I don't know of any true friendship that is bought. But, from an accounting perspective, it would be interesting to see how such "friendships" are quantified.

Just something for us and our state department to consider . . .

&

I have a new-found love for Doris Day. (Google her, then listen to "My Buddy".)

&

"Google it."—The easiest two words that you can use instead of trying to explain a noun.

&

Hello there Sharon Stone: Do you recall you and I playing a four-hand piano arrangement of "Heart and Soul" during your birthday celebration in the Riviera Hotel's penthouse in Las Vegas a few years ago?

I would love to play a four-hand piano duet with you again.

I recall—in fact, I have difficulty in not recalling—that great full-length, split-paneled black skirt you wore that night. You know the one that opened up upon your sitting down at the piano bench. Treasured memories for me . . . but I digress . . .

I do offer to play for you a request selection or two from your favorite Cole Porter songbook. Anytime.

Sharon, do you know what was so brilliant about (our shared appreciation for) Cole Porter's creations? I feel rather certain that you will agree that Cole Porter had that very unique talent to create perfect marriages of music and lyrics in all of his songs.

In fact, few single composers have incorporated such dual-dimensional musical and lyrical combinations in one body of work as did the great Cole Porter.

For example: It could be argued that Bach was essentially a one-dimensional (musical) composer. Same to same: Beethoven, Chopin, Debussy, and on and on . . .

With me so far?

How many great poets also wrote great music? Robert Frost? Walt Whitman? Edgar Allen Poe? For that matter, any Poet Laureate?

Shakespeare?

How about the music and lyrical writing combinations of Rogers and Hammerstein, Elton John and Bernie Tauzin? The Gershwin Brothers? Two people in each case.

You get the point.

And then there are the Mozarts and Wagners of the world who created entire operas consisting of song, drama, dance and staging: An amazing and historically rare entertainment talent.

Today we have the modern three-dimensional musical composers who blend music, lyrics and new technology into their gifts to the world.

To all: Please send me your own examples of those single prodigious artists who have brilliantly blended in the ingredients of music, lyrics, dance, staging and design into one *lasting* musical artistic creation.

David Bowie? Madonna? Trent Reznor? Who else?

Sir Andrew Lloyd Webber—a modern day operetta standout.

But . . . will any of these modern writers mentioned above survive the test of centuries?

&

Batteries: The new plastics.

&

Ain't technology grand?

And can there be anything so damn more frustrating and upsetting when it doesn't work?

&

While I have this opportunity, I've got to tell you about a late, late night in 1969 during which I was playing at Jilly's, on 52nd Street in New York City when Judy Garland walked in.

She sat at the piano bar just a few feet from me, leaned over and very softly and kindly asked me to play the great Johnny Burke and Jimmy Van Heusen's song, "Here's That Rainy Day".

After my set and during our subsequent chat, Ms. Garland asked me if I wouldn't mind if she and her pianist friend, Mickey (whose last name I apologize, but cannot remember) sit in and do a couple of numbers.

It was almost four o'clock on a misty and sultry Sunday night/early Monday morning in New York City. There were only a few customers left in the joint; even fewer employees; and my band members and I, when the great and wonderful international entertainment icon, Ms. Judy Garland sat on the piano bench, took the microphone in hand, and gave us an unforgettably memorable private musical concert.

She started her set with "The Party's Over".

A few days afterwards, we and the world were shocked to hear that Judy Garland had died.

"Here's That Rainy Day" and "The Party's Over" . . .

&

Where is our nation's gold?

Please don't tell me Ft. Knox.

&

Don't we all have those one or two favorite elementary school teachers?

For me, Mrs. Haines, who taught general subjects in the 4th grade; Mr. Sokolove, sports in the 6th grade; Ms. Wood, English and Communications' studies in my 50th grade of education, and Mr. Souder, my piano teacher (thanks for the piano and the lessons, Dad).

Who were your favorites? Which one(s) were inspirational to you? Motivational? Transformational?

And for you teachers of today, which of your teachers were role models to the extent that you were influenced to decide upon entering the profession?

&

While I am on the subject, I just watched a major network television show that focused on school lunches, gang violence and bullying.

What the go-fish happened to education in this country?

&

I want to feel the tangibility of achievement. So do all men and women, but particularly men; it's a guy thing.

&

Food is and will always be the fundamental economic driver. Food.

&

If it were ever to be harnessed and developed, I suggest investing in neutrinos' technology.

The energy is provided free of charge.

&

As a "white guy", I am offended by the current trend of ridiculing my race and gender.—Bruce Westcott

&

In musicians' parlance, my old friend, Wayne Newton, sang his ass off on "Danke Schoen". (". . . ass off on?" Oh well . . .)

And listen to Billy Joel's great writing and vintage singing of "An Innocent Man".

Sorry for confining myself to a certain musical era, but I think that Elton John's writing partner, Bernie Taupin, is the top lyricist of his generation. Elton, of course, is the top musical entertainer of his time. Sure, we can talk about Paul Simon or Sting or Steely Dan or Cold Play and Green Day, or Jay-Z, or Lady Gaga, or Lady Day, or any other artist for that matter regarding their special talents during given certain eras. How about Neil Diamond in his era? Frank Sinatra was the greatest of pop singers, but he rarely wrote either music or lyrics, although I believe that he was imminently capable of being an equally great composer and lyricist. Frank told me that he had a special affinity for the musical composer/lyrist and also for the singer/instrumentalist. Very few people know that Frank Sinatra played the piano. Frank Sinatra realized the importance of reading and writing the language of his choice of profession. The truth is that many guitar players, for example, neither read nor write the language of music.

I attribute that to laziness.

It is the extended-generation artist in any field that impresses me.

My favorite styles of music are Classical, Jazz, and what is known as the Great American Standards, especially, as I said earlier, Cole Porter's brilliant melding of music and lyrics. And I love hearing genuine country music; it brings me memories of my hillbilly-and-proud-of-it grandmother walking around the house singing original Hank Williams' songs. When I was a kid we never missed a Saturday night radio broadcast of "Grand Ole Opry", as our entire family echoed Minnie Pearl's signature salutation, "Just as proud to be here". Great memories.

Staying with some musical notes (couldn't help the pun):

My favorite pianists are Vladimir Horowitz, Artur Rubinstein, Oscar Peterson, Van Cliburn, Joe Sample, Gus Mancuso, Ramsey Lewis, Chick Corea, Ahmad Jamal, Phil Rudy, Lyle May, Monty Alexander, Blair Aaronson, and on and on when hearing the constantly emerging great pianists of our day.

(Put on some Oscar Peterson and listen to a real jazz piano player.)

Brothers, Freddie and Nat "King" Cole, and of course, Ray Charles, were the best pianist/singers. (As Imus would say, I love me some Ray Charles. When I was a kid, I would drag my little brother, Dickie, up to the Royal Theater on Pennsylvania Avenue in Baltimore for those memorable Saturday movie and live music matinees that featured all of the great R&B artists of the day, including Ray and his entire orchestra. Dickie and I sometimes were the only little toe-heads in the theatre, but the only thing that we got pelted with was popcorn that sometimes, I admit, we playfully started. Man, what beautiful times they were.)

Digressing a little in thinking of Pennsylvania Avenue, there was relatively little drug use during those days. Sure, there was a little pot passed around and seemingly one would have to have been a musician or a stage comic (Lenny Bruce comes to mind) to be doing heroin. Cocaine was available in over-the-counter cough medicines (and allegedly in Coca Cola). But for the main part, most of us were really actually afraid of the drugs.

Instead, everybody drank. On the streets, in the alleys, ducking into someone's home or in a store doorway, and always in a brown paper bag. (I don't know exactly who we thought we were fooling; other than ourselves.) But I now question how all that has changed . . .

Pianists, Bob James, Dave Grusin, and Thelonious Monk, and guitarist, Lee Ritenour are the very best of the jazz composers. Grusin and James have the greatest of harmonic sensibility in their compositions and playing.

Gary Graffman is the best of the left-hand-only composition pianists.

Maria Callas is the greatest of all female singers.

Pavarotti is the greatest of male vocalists. Maybe Caruso was the technician, but Luciano was the most expressive of the lot.

Puccini's "Nessun Dorma" is the most thrilling of the operatic melodies, particularly when sung by Pavarotti and Andrea Bocelli. It always gives me chills when I hear the song so beautifully and emotionally sung.

No one—no one—sang a lyric quite like Frank Sinatra.

Rachmaninoff's "Second Piano Concerto in C Minor" is the most stirring and melodic piano concerto of all time (try having sex with that one). Chopin melodies come in a close second in that regard in my opinion. And nothing is more musically thrilling than the opening of Prokofiev's 2nd Piano Concerto.

(Here's a suggestion for you brilliant musical arrangers: Do the Prokofiev 2nd opening with a combination of instruments, climaxing at the top of the opening with a feedback guitar track. Whew!!!)

Getting back to music and sex: In the hands of Rachmaninoff and Chopin, sex transforms into passionate love.

Tom Petty, Sting, Carole King and James Taylor exemplify the best combination of a writer, singer, instrumentalist and performer in popular music.

Cold Play, Green Day, and The Killers rule the day.

Art Blakey and that guy playing now for Paul McCartney are the best drummers.

The Beatles are in a category of their own.

Seeing some of the re-runs on PBS Television, I think that there was some great musicianship going on on the Lawrence Welk Show (and some talented and good-looking men and women.)

I do appreciate trumpeter Miles Davis' talent, but I do resent his statement that Jazz is a "black man's music". First of all, musical improvisation dates back centuries throughout "white man's music". And Mr. Davis really ought to take into consideration that the very instrument that he mastered was invented by white men.

I think that Stevie Wonder's "As" is the greatest Pop song ever written. And I think that Stevie's "Living For The City" and Marvin Gay's "Heard It Through The Grapevine" are the greatest R&B songs of all time.

David Foster, Bert Bacharach and Carole King: Great modern composers.

Sir Elton and Bernie Taupin's "Take Me To The Pilot" rivals Queen and Pink Floyd in symphonic orchestrations of the rock and roll repertoire.

And don't you love hearing Keith Jarrett's improvisations go off the range, or laying it all down in the pocket, as musicians would say.

One of the windfall benefits in studying music (I studied privately with a Peabody Conservatory music professor, Richard Aiken) is that one's appreciation of outstanding musical talent is greatly enhanced. I know it when I hear great musicianship (one of the assets that Caesars Palace's Cliff Perlman recognized in appointing me as his entertainment chief).

(A note to some critics of my musical performances: I know, far more so than you and others of my own musical limitations.)

Frank Sinatra and I privately discussed how much our piano studies enhanced our appreciation for all art. Pretty bright guy, that Mr. Frank Sinatra. Do many of us realize his entrepreneurial talents? His management and leadership skills? The qualities of his personally selected board of directors? His investments? His designs? His paintings? Frank's staging abilities? Frank Sinatra could conduct an orchestra: All of which were no easy feats, and none of which seemingly have been broadly recognized—until now.

Rap music, particularly Jay-Z's, is highly-creatively produced. Credit technology.

It is hard for me to embrace white rock music of the 60's and 70's after listening throughout my teen years to authentic 50's R&B music. I can tell 99% of the time if I am listening to a white or a black musical artist, including instrumentalists (It's in the feeling of the musical expression of this category of musical artists). And the new trend of white entertainers adopting the black stage style and gestures (crotch-holding for example) of blacks is ridiculous, embarrassing and demeaning. I'd bet that black artists feel the same.

Listen and observe for yourself and tell me about your thoughts on the subject and express your musical preferences, and why.

And yes, it is true that I have played and sung at many private parties at my favorite musical entertainer of all time, Frank Sinatra's, home in Palm Springs, California. (As you can imagine, the guest lists were sometimes amazing and always diverse.)

For me, it was a very cool experience, for example, sitting in Frank Sinatra's private living room, fireplace roaring, an Oscar gracing a shelf, photos of movie star ex-wives on tables, and listening to a reel-to-reel un-released sample recording of "My Way".

&

(A shout out to my black friends: You are missing out on some truly incredible music from the world of Classical Music that many of you disparagingly refer to as "White Music".)

&

How many of you received all of those rebate checks on products that you bought and sent in based on the advertised price?

And when was the last time that you received a full box of cereal or bag of potato chips?

&

We've been told that God made man in His image.

I do not think so and here is why:

First of all, for man to make such an assertion defines the lengthy extent of arrogance and conceit.

Which man? The infant man? The adolescent man? The teen man, the young adult, the middle-aged man? The older man?

I defy such a ridiculous claim by simply placing 100 photographs of infants in one contiguous row and 100 images of older men in another row, then present a challenge to accurately match the babies' countenances to the old guys. Hell, we can hardly match 100 photographs of wartime service men in their 20's with men in their later years.

And secondly, God is a woman.

Think about it: Even the Immaculate Conception was borne by a woman.

You guys discuss this one. I'm already convinced.

&

If we did drill that hole to China, wouldn't that tip the Earth's axis?

Fly me to the moon . . .

&

The new version of a Paul Reverse warning:

One if by land line; two if by cellular.

&

We've got to have wishful thinking. We've got to dream, we've got to at least reach for the stars, right?

&

I say string up bicycle thieves.

Well . . . former Las Vegas Mayor, Oscar Goodman, wants to cut off the thumbs of graffiti "taggers".

Actually and through an experience of having lived and worked as a ranch hand for a while in Searchlight, Nevada (Sen. Harry Reidville), I would prefer to throw those thieving rats into a pit of cactus. And don't even get me started on those bicycle thieves.

&

I muse sometimes about how joyous it is to swig the juice from a freshly cut orange while standing in the middle of a Florida or California orange grove on a hot day.

&

I ponder the question of why has God provided human beings with such a variety of nourishments. We humans have so many options to satisfy even the basic requirements of sustaining our lives.

We separate out other species in terms and categories of vegetarians and carnivores. For example, Lions and tigers don't want to hear nothin' about no' vegetables . . . .

So is that the reason we humans have been given the various and discernible senses? Is it for us to sometimes casually and cavalierly browse and select from among our food choices? Today, we call that selection process grocery shopping. And it seems that we are continuously discovering new and usually delicious plants, roots and vegetables from around the world.

Why is it that most species, particularly animal species, have various and superior-to-us degrees of the senses? Are those diverse levels of the senses God-given or are they the result of an evolutionary development carried out through the generational challenges of survival?

In fact, why do we need nourishment at all? Why can't we just exist and die? We often question the reason for life; for what purpose does death serve either God or us?

We'll touch on this and other related questions throughout this book.

For example: Why does God make so many things in life so difficult?

The answer: "Sometimes God challenges us."—Bruce Westcott

&

What goes on in those Universal black holes? Some scientists and assorted other observers say that nothing goes on in black holes. I disagree. It is obvious to me that *some* sort of physics exists inside black holes.

Logical reasoning: *Something* has to keep whatever it is inside of those black holes suspended and relatively stable.

Speaking of Quantum Mechanics, it makes sense to me that *something* must exist between quantum leaps. Can something ride the rail of nothing?

There obviously is so much in the universe that exists way outside of our current realm of abilities to measure.

What are your questions regarding our Universe?

&

If humans do evolve, what would the next long-term stages of human development/evolution consist of?

For example: Would we grow wings to fly? ("Fly Away"— A 1970's song written and recorded by Bruce Westcott, produced by Michael Yerman)

Would we evolve to further unlocking of the human brain? If so, what wondrous developments will such an expansion of the brain subsequently be invented?

(You know that the U. S. Patent Office once declared—I think that it was during the 1920's—that all things that can be invented *had* been invented.)

And if such an unlocking of the brain were to occur, what new understandings would be revealed? Would there be new revelations into unknown dimensions, the spiritual dimension, which I am convinced, exists, for example?

&

What is spirituality?

Whatever it truly is, I believe that we are finally evolving to becoming capable of entering into and engaging the realm of spirituality.

There are many documented cases of spiritual breakthroughs. Isn't that so, Art Bell?

&

Does the scientific String Theory have an unknown and/or therefore undiscovered spiritual factor?

Professor Michio Kaku: What do you think of this question?

&

Is premonition a dimension that we instinctively enter into?

(Did Judy Garland have a premonition on that night at Jilly's?)

It seems to me that both instinct and premonition have to be opened and entered into through—for lack of a better word—a dimension.

Or perhaps are these portals in or from yet another dimension? If so and in which case the question arises: Are there layers of dimensions?

To my mind, the subject of the existence of a set of unknown dimensional theories is easily proved by recent technological developments that expand upon the currently understood human senses. Reminding you that modern scientists have actually developed products based on the discoveries of senses within other species, such as rattlesnakes and platypuses.

Therefore, If senses can be scientifically duplicated from other species (or logically and eventually from within ourselves), why then can we not technologically enter into other dimensions?

Is there in a clue for our space experiments?

If ever we were to break through the barriers into other dimensions, it seems scientifically logical that therein is the pathway to all sorts of travel whether it is past, future, distance, etc.

To quote Judy Tenuta, "It could happen".

&

Here's a fun proposition for you to ponder:

I wonder just how extraterrestrial life describes to one another the Earth and its strange and fascinating inhabitants. Discuss . . .

&

And here's a little fun pause in your day for you:

Say" twitter-tweet" ten times real fast.

Now challenge your friends.

How did you do, Ellen?

&

A question for you mad scientists out there:

Which is faster: light or time? See the correct answer provided elsewhere in this book.

Check your watches. On the basis of perception, time is moving much more rapidly relative to only 100 years ago. Will evolution and its development catch up with the speed of time? Will perception ever become part of the equation? If not, why not? Do all things have a relativity component to consider when formulating scientific theories?

&

The entire Universe is violent. So, why then is it such a surprise that all earthly beings are also violent?

Does the main underlying reason for such basic violence come down to hunger? Keep in mind that some of what we call violent behavior, most animals, birds and insects refer to as preparing for dinner.

And keep in mind that humans are among the minority of earthly species that kill for the sake of killing. We're the civilized species? How does that make sense?

If hunger were the case, is the Universe "hungry" for its own sources of nourishment?

Does the Universe require a feeding of its appetite in order to expand? Is it the Pac Man theory? Would that not be tantamount to the basic principle of (Universal) cannibalism?

Isn't cannibalism natural? It is if you get stuck on a snowy mountaintop in the Andes. How about after a nuclear disaster? "How do you like your balls", said the chef, "steamed, boiled or fried?"

Oh settle down, I'm just having a little fun.

There is a related relativity theory that I could get behind, such as when things and events take on a new or different explanation relative to or in relation to changing circumstances.

Or is everything relative to or in relation to everything?

Is it a sensibly intertwined Universe?

I have my own Theory of Relativity, which is encapsulated with the following comparative analysis:

If I spend five bucks for something and Warren Buffet spends fifty (or, in Ebonics, it is fity) grand for something, in terms of comparative wealth and spending it is all relative.

&

Scientists tell us that the Universe is continuously expanding. Okay, I accept that. However, I question for what reason(s) or cause(s), and what "nourishes" its expansion? What is the objective? Is there an objective?

It's just expanding? That's all? For what purpose? For the purpose of expanding? Huh?

Is the expansion of the universe God's intent?

Or has She seen Her creation of the Universe thing get out of hand?

In either case, keep in mind that most living things in the universe expand. Humans, as do most species on Earth, expand from birth. And then once we reach a point to which the physical aspect of that expansion process can expand no further, we begin the process of deterioration. And then we die. As of right now, that makes absolutely no sense to me whatsoever.

I guess that we'll just to wait for these answers the same way that (I hope) we will be enlightened as to all the mysteries of the Universe, which is, of course, upon entering the fabled and mysterious world of . . . shutter to say it: Death.

What is death? Is there an eventual finality to everything? There's that relativity factor again.

Another perplexing question for us to ponder prior to our death is whether or not we will have to pass through a series of awareness stages and challenges in order for us to be enlightened to all of those mysterious riddles of the Universe. Or do the dimensions, and God Herself, reveal themselves immediately upon the passage of life to death?

Or . . . will we experience a Geraldo Rivera moment of finding nothing?

&

Why did God make human breasts so sexually sensitive?

And why, and for what purpose, did God make nipples on men?

I don't get it, but Gore Vidal claims that male nipple sensitivity proves his theory that all humans are inherently bi-sexual.

&

At no time in our nation's history have we had three consecutively worse presidents than Clinton, Bush, and Obama.

&

Are you as impressed and affected as much as I am while reading the eloquence that was contained among the heart and brain-touching letters written during the Civil War?

Not just from high ranking, sometimes, but not always, educated commanders, but particularly from the hearts and pens of simple, but not simply, battlefield soldiers.

And could there ever have been more of a concentration of written eloquence than that which were so well articulated and exchanged between our nation's founding fathers and mothers?

And would their today's e-mail exchanges contain crap, such as u r or LOL? Or little smilies? I could see Jefferson joshing it up a bit with a smilie tagged on the sweeping end of his signature.

Speaking of Jefferson, I understand that there is a movement afoot in the political correctness community of this country to remove references of greatness relative to Thomas Jefferson on the basis that he was a "slave owner". (Keep in mind that the winners write the history books, so don't discount the possibility that Thomas Jefferson will be ignored in future American history books—not if, but when the left completely takes over this country.)

Now they're saying that Thomas Jefferson is not worthy of our national praise for his rather significant role in accomplishing no small feat such as forming the United States of America on the basis that Mr. Jefferson owned slaves. And that he spied upon his slaves.

No. and Not.

Mr. Jefferson was managing his sprawling, well-earned and maintained and profitable estate by observing his investment in what was regarded in its time as being part of his portfolio of assets, and from which his observations he no doubt made improvements. Mr. Jefferson was also no doubt aware of the importance in maintaining the physical condition of his work force.

They were fed, clothed, housed and cared for medically. They were not chained and beaten. They had their periods of recreation and time off during which they procreated and created the basis for all American dance and Pop music.

All of which is no less similar to today's political slave environment.

I say that if one is enslaved to money, he and she are nonetheless enslaved.

34

&

My God, what a shameful heap of wasted brilliant minds is the result of wars. Look, for example, during one speck of recent time during World War II. How many Einsteins . . .?

Do you realize that the Second World War and its atrocities occurred only 70 years ago? Do you think that during a mere 70 years of human history, we humans have evolved to such a dramatic extent that war and human atrocities have been erased from our psychic?

If you do think so, do you wanna' buy a bridge?

&

Of course, the same question could be applied to any war and at any point in human history.

I must have a dozen or so additional thoughts on this subject written and stored somewhere. I'm sure you have some thoughts on the subject.

There is so much to be discussed on the subject of war isn't that so?

Primarily: Is war the Great Debate?

&

Speaking of debates:

It is interesting to note that the racial debates of the American Civil War continue to rage. Of course it does. Race is a tribal thing. Tribal differences are inherently either territorial, as is with mostly all Earthly species, or, in the case of humans, centered on racial or political philosophical tribal differences.

It is also interesting to note that in most species other than humans, the hierarchies have long since been designed and settled by nature.

The remaining lesser intelligent, in my opinion, species establish themselves through combat.

And it is said that humans have evolved?

Unfortunately, and until that brain expansion idea kicks in that is referenced elsewhere within this tome, racial debates and subsequent conflicts shall continue to be timeless and endless.

Religions are an entirely different matter . . .

&

Another interesting fantasy proposition for us to think about is to envision and then analyze what the consequences of war, or even certain historical battles, would have been and would exist today had the other side of those conflicts won.

My brother, Dickie, wrote a brilliant anecdotal scenario in which he imagined what the ultimate consequences would be if Hitler and Churchill (instead of Hitler and Mussolini) had become European allies.

&

Ancient man has always answered in the affirmative as to the question of whether or not spiritual and/or extraterrestrial life exists elsewhere in our Universe. Proof: They prayed.

And they prayed because they knew it, folks; they saw it, they experienced it and they retold those experiences generationally. And their prayers were specifically directed to the great and superior otherworldly visitors.

Look for the return . . .

"Spooky", said Einstein.

&

So what? It is feared that upon an U.S. exit from Afghanistan, the Taliban or the Iranians would exert themselves upon the Afghanistan people. Rubbish. The Afghanistan people can take care of themselves, thank you very much.

Haven't you noticed, you dense State Department advisors and officials, it's Afghanistan! Afghans like their ancient lifestyle of tribalism, donkeys and caves. And they really don't seem to mind the warring—as long as it's between themselves.

The Afghan person, as do the now-confirmed Iraqi people, merely tolerates the presence of the current allied military occupation based purely on respect for the military might. And they don't seem to mind receiving the $billion handouts . . .

By the way, how are those poppy fields doing over there? Drug War my ass.

I have always warned that we not go there. And I have continuously suggested that we get the hell out of there. Frustratingly, I've joined with the majority of American citizens who piss in the wind regarding expressing our views on these, the latest of our two wars.

America's enemies had better double up on their praying if I were to become the President of the United States. I have proven to have no compunction to pull the trigger in the defense of my family, my land, my country, and myself. And I fight and play to win! There'd be no more patty-cake wars for this country.

(Those of you who are politically-interested readers should read my Internet post titled, "What's the big deal?", regarding the Mr. Obama big bail-outs. I'll save you some time: I opposed the Iraq and Afghanistan wars and the Wall St. bailouts.)

Oh how we need to inject/infuse/instill/and implement some sensibility into our government!

&

I love the Jewish people.

I am in awe of their resiliency and tenacity.

I admire their superior-level intelligence; I concur with their claim to ancient lands; and I greatly appreciate and respect their acumen throughout a wide and diverse range of historical accomplishments.

&

I am the guy who had originally suggested that every single personal United States' debt that exists within the international banking system, excluding personal loans between individuals and business loans, be immediately wiped out and written off.

All mortgages and credit card debt forgiven. Write it off, Mr. Banker, and re-start your (reformed) loan practices from scratch.

Banks and investment firms will get over it. They have plenty of money with which to start all over.

Talk about economic stimulus: Think of the spectacular stimulation to manufacturing, jobs and housing that would impact the United States' economy by the single stroke of a presidential pen.

Read more about this and other sensible solutions that are outlined in my presidential candidacy platform, "Formula for America" (Source: brucewestcott.org)

&

Let them eat oil!—Bruce Westcott

Oil is a <u>commodity</u>. As such, America and Americans have a choice of buying a world-market commodity or developing our own energy sources, and yes, including drilling our own oil wells.

(At least until which time we wean ourselves from oil dependency, which doesn't mean that in the meantime we can't have trade—fair trade—with oil-producing nations.)

It has been suggested that America has been held by the throat by oil-producing nations. Duh! If I am being held by the throat, I think that I would know it and DO something about it. And in that context, if I were the President of the United States, nations that hold our nation by the throat would get a swift uppercut from the ground up.

Let's see how much corn, wheat and cattle can be raised in sand, if you catch my drift.

&

Here's a voting concept for you to ponder:

Have the President instruct the Federal Elections Commission (FEC) to provide a write-in option on Federal election ballots in all 50 states and territories.

(This would *not* violate the Tenth Amendment to the United States Constitution.)

Why is it that modern Americans are forced to vote within the restrictions of a two-party political party system instead of having a national write-in option for a citizen's personal choice of who they want to be elected to Federal government offices?

Won't happen you say? I say, with apologies to President Kennedy, why not? Are we not talking about OUR federal government and the vastly important, needed and trusted leadership of our nation?

Well then, just as we ought not be held by the throat by other nations, nor should we be held by the throat by the two-party system—or in any other respect for that matter by the President and the Congress of the United States. Isn't the basic purpose for having elections to elect a President and a Congress that represents The People?

Voting is a right; a real entitlement belonging to us citizens <u>only</u>. And as such, American citizens ought to be able to vote for whomever we choose to represent us in public office.

Pointing out that, constitutionally, to resist and abolish such a narrow-minded and subjective restraint of our voting rights is protected and guaranteed in our Declaration of Independence. It is the Democratic way, isn't it? Okay then, let's revolt against such a repression by our government.

And then we'll work on ensuring unambiguous voting accuracy; we'll move our voting tabulation system back to the United States; and jail those who would defraud any aspect of our voting system.

&

Another comparative analysis for your consideration:

Alexander the Great's forcibly-conscripted Persian-infused armies vis a vis America's forcibly-conscripted (they call it "training") Iraq and Afghanistan armies.

The grammatically-incorrect conclusion in both instances: It don't work.

&

Now compare the following societies and cultures:

Japan's tsunami wipe-out and restoration vis a vis Haiti's recent similar circumstances and (wasted) $billion re-building results; Israel's enslaved and persecuted Jews with African enslavement and persecution.

I am merely presenting the facts for your consideration. You reach your own conclusions.

&

I have no desire to dine with radio talk show host, Michael Savage. He constantly slobbers and sniffles. I once called his program producer and asked that tissue paper be provided to Dr.Savage during his broadcasts. But Michael is totally correct about much of his observations regarding our government and our military.

Same to same with that Neil Cavuto-ass-kissing, definitively-arrogant, and constantly-baby-like-thumb-pacifier-sucking-whining-and-pouting-gut-sucking-worm, Don Imus, whose radio program is a must-have with my morning coffee.

Who could take it (unpaid that is)?

First of all, Mr. Imus, we're all going to die, so get over it cowboy.

And, Mr. Imus, please don't respond to my observations about your otherwise brilliant sorry-ass with that punch-you-in-the-mouth horseshit of yours. I might take you up on that.

&

Author's note: Although the following text was originally noted prior to the Occupy Wall St. demonstrations, there is at least a certain amount of basic trueness that is simultaneously emerging in my following warning to those of you who are rich or think that you are financially secure:

Don't kid yourself. And, in that context, do not allow your cavalier attitudes and self-deception to think that you can't lose it all.

For example: How are those 401k, and Madoff and Corzine investments working out for some of you?

And, do you think that just because you worked all of your life to pay off your home, you now think that you own it? Try not paying your taxes and see what happens to "your" home.

Has Congress stolen your Social Security investment money, Bunkie?

You ain't alone.

For example, I went from over three decades of a modestly successful career, including a 14-year run as a featured performer on Cleopatra's Barge at Caesars Palace. I then became a big-shot Executive Producer of Entertainment at the Dune's Hotel/Casino and Country Club in Las Vegas. After that I became an owner/operator of a Florida-based fast food restaurant concept, the Great American Hot Dog and Draught Beer Emporiums. I had a forward plan to build 100 stores upon which to then build my own hotel/ casino in Las Vegas—following the successful model that Cliff Perlman's family established when they built Lum's, a Florida-based hot dog chain, which they then leveraged in order to purchase Caesars Palace for $60 million (that's with an m, not a b). (At the time of the sale, Cliff was laughed at;

I know, I was sitting in the same restaurant booth with the sellers during the laugh fest).

From there, and based on an entire range of valuable lessons learned from my business experiences, I became Chairman of a Nevada-based casino acquisition corporation whose Board of Directors consisted of three former presidents of publicly-traded gaming corporations, including a corporate counsel who, at the time, was advising the Bank of Moscow.

Our (my) corporation was represented by the top gaming legal firm in Nevada: Jones, Jones, Close and Brown; and our due diligence was conducted through the professional services of the internationally leading hotel and casino accounting firm, Laventhol & Horwath.

I had definitively, according to gorilla marketing principles, positioned myself to ultimately become a billionaire.

Instead, I became homeless.

As that great sage, Whoopie Goldberg said: "Careers can go up and careers can go down".

As a side note: Casino developer, Steve Wynn, should thank his lucky stars that I did not succeed in my quest to acquire the old Aladdin Hotel and Casino.

Reason: Had I been successful in obtaining the Aladdin, the Las Vegas Strip would have developed differently. Based on what I believe would have been an imminent financial success with the Aladdin, I would have suggested to our board that we start our planned long-term growth by purchasing the Dunes Hotel/Casino (where I once held a successful top executive position). Our group would have then enclosed both ends of the Dunes' golf course property with the acquisition of the NW corner of Tropicana Avenue and Las Vegas Boulevard (present site of the New York, New York hotel/casino).

Only the poorly and blandly designed newer tower at the Dune's would have been imploded entirely instead of leveling the entire property, as did Steve Wynn. Our group had a vision to gut the interior of the original old hotel structure and give it balconies, a redesigned open penthouse cocktail lounge and outdoor observation deck, and wrap the entire concept around a Miami Beach and South Shore golf and water themed hotel/casino and country club attraction.

The new Dunes was planned to include top of the line amenity attractions, such as the World's Greatest Nightclub; a two-story glassed-in steak and jazz bar; a huge aquarium-featured seafood restaurant, and lots of other attractions surrounding and directly impacting the casino areas. This was way before Steve Wynn's vision.

The Dunes' golf course and country club acreage would have been redesigned to include a range of its own attractions, such as private apartment-size guest towers, water and sanctuary attractions and an outdoor concert venue.

The current Mediterranean-themed Bellagio would have eventually and similarly been built, but ours would have been internationally featured at nearby Lake Las Vegas, but admittedly not with as much pizzazz as that which Mr. Wynn provided in his designs. However, we would have had a Pablo Picasso and Dale Chihuly-inspired lobby that were conceived prior to Mr. Wynn's announcement of ideas for the Bellagio (I still have proof of all of the design drafts and exchanges of business correspondence with Lake Las Vegas' Henry Gluck).

But alas, Mr. Wynn, you prevailed on that one. Congratulations. You did well. You are an admired historical hotel developer.

Actually, Steve, I am not jealous. You earned it. But I am envious.

I am an emerging hotel developer, and as such I am properly positioned and prepared for such an exciting venture.

I can look back in recalling that Steve Wynn and I shared the same "think big" advice from Caesars' Cliff Perlman.

Perhaps I was more heavily influenced by Cliff's leadership philosophies than Mr. Wynn, but I think that, based on my observations, Cliff saw in Steve Wynn some sort of partnership potential. So, in consideration that some of these factors were happening during a time in which Cliff had removed himself to a tennis life in Beverly Hills, I believe that it would have been natural for Steve Wynn and I to have eventually engaged in some degree of discussion regarding the events of the day that conceivably could have led to a joint venture hotel/casino project. In this context, please keep in mind that I am talking about the prevailing conditions of the day.

P. S. Of course I am writing a separate book about these and other such experiences during my ride on the elevator of life. And yes, as a definitive entrepreneur, I am hoping that the book is financially successful. My philosophy is that we all have a book in us, but few of us actually write the book.

You can purchase in-house style advance limited first edition collector's item copies of my photos-included memoirs for fifty bucks, personally signed by request.

Just log into brucewestcott.org and order your advance copy.

(Always be the entrepreneur.)

&

On a somewhat related note: I know what casino developer Steve Wynn's secret ingredient is for success. Except for what I pay attention to in the news, I don't know a whole lot about the guy personally, although we did briefly meet on a couple of occasions. I have also criticized Steve Wynn on a couple of occasions.

For example, I once wrote to Mr. Wynn regarding the strategic blunder of his failure to acquire the southwest corner property at the intersection of Las Vegas Boulevard and Tropicana Avenue. That property would have been a relatively minor, but sensibly strategic financial investment that would have attached his Dunes' country club property(now the Bellagio) to both ends of the entire length of Las Vegas Boulevard from Flamingo Road to Tropicana Avenue.

Instead, my friend from my Jilly's in Palm Springs, California days, Kirk Kerkorian, purchased that corner property from a Japanese firm that didn't quite know or understand what to do with it. (I wished Kirk Kerkorian a Happy and Healthy New Year's Eve1999/2000 at the Bellagio in Las Vegas, a conversation in which Kirk and I lamented the loss of "the boys", in Kirk Kerkorian's words, referring to Frank and Jilly and others of that era that we sadly and regrettably lost.)

(Interesting to note that all four of the recent Japanese owners of Las Vegas hotel/casinos have failed. You Las Vegas pundits and observers: Discuss.)

The afore-mentioned Tropicana Avenue property is now the location of the New York, New York Hotel and Casino.

Even Steve Wynn has had his wouda', couda', shouda' moments in his illustrious career.

Getting back to Mr. Wynn's secret ingredient that is necessary for all business success:

Three early lessons that I learned from my own small business experience and gleaned from that of my personal discussions with former Caesars' Chairman, Cliff Perlman, is that: 1) everything in business is built on a rule of paying attention to the details; 2) that details are the building blocks of a successful business foundation; and 3) that a developer has the responsibility to arrange those building blocks sensibly and properly aligned to the business intent and vision.

Details, details, details: Steve Wynn's Secret Ingredient to a Successful Business Endeavor. And that it all has to look, feel, sound and taste—Steve Wynn's word—delicious. (I like the insertion of that word, Steve.)

And now, my business advice:

Other than the obvious necessity of learning the details of your own business endeavors, I think it is necessary in achieving your success that you follow the fundamental principle of having a hands-on experience in your chosen field of enterprise.

"It's the fundamentals."—Vince Lombardi

Also, you must fully understand your market. In that respect, you must delve into all aspects of your business endeavor in order to further understand the purchasing psychic of your targeted market. What is your targeted market thinking? What do they want and what will satisfy that want and desire? And in bottom-line summary, what will drive that thinking, that want, and eventually them, to your product?

That, and pricing of your product or service is equally important to your success. Some products, for example, are intentionally priced within a low-end bracket marketing strategy; usually the-lower-the-better for volume-based selling, while there are other products whose quality and *psychological* marketing strategies require that they be priced higher so as to create an image of exclusivity and desirability within a targeted sales' range.

Pricing is an unruly and tricky aspect of any successful management of a product or service. So be careful in your pricing; pricing could prick you.

"The Quality of Details and Market Understanding to A Successful Business Venture"—The working title for another forthcoming book from Bruce Westcott

&

I can only imagine Donald Trump's wealth if he had listened to my numerous pleas and plans to develop Las Vegas hotel/casinos.

Check it out, Mr. Trump, I speak the truth.

&

DoubleMySpeed.com qualifies for one of broadcasting's Greatest Radio Commercial of All Time. The radio spots mention their product over 25 times. Try to pull that off, Madison Avenue.

&

Cats and Dogs:

I wonder why big cats eat us and small cats just want to snuggle with us.

Most certainly in that sense, size matters.

Have you ever noticed that after a night of horrendous cat noises, the next day the cats are running or lounging around with nary a visible scratch?

Is it possible that those seemingly vicious battle sounds are maybe, shall we say, different than from our human interpretation?

Are the cats fighting or making love? That is the question. (I've known some scratching and howling cat women in my life. But, yes, that is a subject that most of you do not care to know about.)

Have you ever seen a roaming pack or similar formation of cats? You will with dogs.

I was recently intrigued by my neighborhood cats that had almost immediately sensed the death of my dear 15-year old German Shepard/wolf-mix, Sky Boy.

Do cats have a spiritual sense of death? If not then is it the pervading odor that indicates the finality of death? Of course there is a decomposition process of any animal that passes, but the death of Sky Boy was discovered by cats within a mere few hours of his passing.

In fact, the neighborhood cats were all but doing a dance on my property, boldly prancing around in possible celebration of Sky Boy's passing. For sure, they were establishing their own territorial boundaries.

Ah, animal instincts . . .

We bond with cats and dogs in particular for a variety of reasons. First of which is that they bond with us and we like that.

Cuteness, playmates, companionship, loyalty (not cats) . . . could be among the various reasons of explanation for the bonding factors between certain animals and us dumb humans.

I say dumb humans on account of dogs being the more intelligent communicators between themselves and humans. Proof: Dogs understand human language, but you go and try to figure out what a dog's bark is saying . . . just saying . . .

Cats' purrs and meows are understandable for the most part, but when was the last time that your cat obeyed your verbal commands? And do you not follow their commands? Just asking . . .

Is the separation between small and large cats defined by meows, and hisses and growls?

Just saying . . .

Whether or not most of us are aware of it, cats and dogs closely observe us. Some of us they trust; some of them are skeptical of us. We often fascinate them. We perplex them. We pick up huge items, such as trash cans and our babies, and we can throw them around at will, sometimes with different intentions such as while under the contrasting influences of playfulness or anger. We ride away and arrive back in some sort of contraption on something we humans shrug off as merely being wheels. Meanwhile, cats and dogs wait for us during our absences and only wonder what we are going to bring back to eat, and why and what was so important that they couldn't have gone off with us. (I think that it must be that cats and dogs assume that when we leave home, we are merely going off on a hunting trip that sometimes, but not always, yields some consumable reward for their patient waiting.)

"How do they do that?", these animals of natural, therefore higher intelligence must wonder about us. Our pets somehow communicate to each other of their amazement and fascination with us humans and the very strange things that we do.

Speaking of strange behavior, why is it that 2 dogs, or 2 cocks, or 2 tarantulas, or 2 bears, or a minimum of two each from some species of nature such as cute little birds (not really, they are vicious little creatures) and insects, and so forth, can be put into an enclosure together that results in deathly battle, yet put 2 cats together under the same conditions and usually only a soft meow results?

It has been proven that even wild turkeys possess more natural intelligence than we humans do.

And although we humans unselfishly provide food and shelter to our pets, there is one particularly common trait between them and us, which is that they partly reciprocate by providing one another with hugs and kisses.

&

Here's a dozen of rhyming modern slogans pro and con gay for your consideration:

Gay's okay.

Or . . . Gay is okay.

Or . . . Gays are okay.

Or . . . Being gay's okay.

Or . . . Be gay. It's okay.

Or . . . Gay: It's okay.

Or . . . It's okay to be gay.

Or . . . It ain't okay to be gay.

Or . . . Gay: It ain't okay.

Or . . . Gay isn't okay.

Or . . . It ain't easy being gay.

Or . . . Be happy, be gay.

As I said, I'm just having a little fun . . .

&

So let's talk:

First of all, I find it interesting that seemingly most gay men, particularly younger gay men, are good-looking to a point that is considered "gorgeous" by women. "What a shame; what a waste", the women lament.

Psychologists will probably tell us that, with men, it's all a narcissistic thing.

Whereas most outright lesbian women, particularly "dyke" women, are generally unattractive to most men. (Maybe that's why so many unattractive women are drawn to lesbianism.)

I intend no disrespect or rude criticism; I am expressing my observations in generalities.

Bi-sexuality in men and women is an entirely different subject.

But, to my point: I am of the belief that we are all God's children. It makes sense to me that God would at least accept, if not condone, homosexuality within certain levels of the human behavior.

Monkeys seemingly have no problem with homosexuality.

Personally, I do not approve of the concept of licensed marriage between same-sex persons despite having my own understanding and compassion in the matter and my numerous friendships with "gay" people. But who the hell am I to preach and rail on that strange phenomenon of

God-given sexuality? Sex itself is entirely weird enough as it is, isn't it?

In fact, neither do I approve of the licensing requirements for the marriage of individuals. The marriage license is a bunch of bureaucratic crap heaped upon us for the past couple of centuries. Wouldn't it be enough for an officiator of a wedding to verbally declare and to then, if needed, issue a signed proclamation of the marriage?

That said, I do believe that in America, the Land of The Free, any marriage or physical engagement between individuals and what consenting adults do in the supposed privacy of their bedrooms is none of my damn business. And by the same token, those same circumstances ought not to be of any concern relative to the operations of any government.

Do you really think that any one of us, or government in particular, should be standing guard or peering into someone's bedroom?

How about toilets?

&

Separately, but related to the above:

It is worth noting that not since the eras of the Roman and Greek empires and the legendary Babylonian period, has homosexuality been so broadly accepted socially.

Same to same, promiscuity.

Question: Is there a parallel warning contained in this observation?

So then, what is it that is said about learning from our historical pasts?

&

Is there any doubt that Islam and Islamic culture is swallowing the world?

Hint: The Middle East and Africa, and increasingly in America and Europe, are already digested.

Will you be a Sunni or Shiite?

And once that dispute is settled, will there be *anything* left on Earth?

&

"Hey you frogs out there: You people get out of that pond."

Preposterous?

Okay then, consider my thesis regarding a recent Supreme Court, First Amendment ruling:

We are human beings having human experiences. Are you with me on that point?

To describe our human experience, we categorize ourselves and therefore identify ourselves with the simple term, we are people, or in the case of our founding documents, we declare ourselves as being We the People.

Where, or by what decree by any document or stretch of imagination, have we declared ourselves as We The Corporation?

We tell ourselves that we are people. We say that we are persons. And we go as far to say that we are individuals. We exist in a life form of human existence. As such, we are subjected to a highly unique emotional experience called life. Some of us conduct ourselves within a concept of acceptable human behavior; some not. But all of us humans are unquestionably living beings. Right? Still with me?

Dear Supreme Court Justices: Corporations are not living beings/aka people. Period. Corporations cannot possibly be, by any stretch of argument or speculation, considered, construed, or interpreted as being a living being that we call people, Godly or otherwise.

The Supreme Court ruling by a group of nine people who claim that a corporation is a person, and therefore on that basis, they claim, is protected by the Constitutional First Amendment simply based on the merits of their juxtaposition of speech that *they* find to be equivalent to financial transfers, is a distorted assumption.

Sure, corporations and unions consist of groups, or a group, of people, but surely also a corporation or a union is not a *person*. Corporations and unions are entities that surely exist and they are comprised of a group of people, but how in the world can unions and corporations and businesses, or dollar bills for that matter, even remotely be considered a being "people"?

Of course, corporate representation—representation is a keyword—agrees with the SCOTUS decision. It allows for corporate political control over our Republic that is dominated by money, and on that basis alone, the recent SCOTUS ruling on the First Amendment that equates corporations to human beings ought to be struck down, down, down, now, now, now.

(See my Moneyacracy comment.)

The SCOTUS ruling on the First Amendment serves the corporations to the extent that it is the corporations that continue to exert political and operational <u>control</u> over OUR nation. And here I was, under the impression that I live in the United States of America, a REPUBLIC!

Furthermore, to make a long point longer, nowhere is it written or even considered in that declaration called the Constitution of the United States is the word, corporation. And the only reference in the Constitution to a union is that which describes our nation's desire to form "a more perfect union". That, friends, is an entirely different meaning of the same word as so much of our lexicon can be confusing to the unenlightened and improperly educated.

The word, union, as used in the context of the wording of our Constitution, cannot be passed off as being comparable or even similar in the same context of what former President Clinton asked regarding what the meaning of is, is. Wasn't *that* a good one?

It's all politics . . . and it's all political bullshit.

That said: It is also my belief that the First Amendment, as well as the Second Amendment and the Fourteenth Amendments need to be re-written. And I advocate for having the XVI Amendment and its excessive guidebook, The Tax Code, to be simultaneously abolished.

(In this book I outline a better solution to achieve equality, fairness and accountability over any other taxation plan that is being offered in today's terms.)

If those Constitutional Amendments are so clear, why is it that they are subjected to interpretation? I say re-write them concisely (pithily, a word that Bill O'Reilly likes to interject during conversations) and therefore requiring no interpretation by any group of nine or more or less people.

(Sorry, can't help this: Should nine corporations or unions replace the Supreme Court in order to determine these rulings? If you think so then please tell me what a corporation or union looks like particularly seated on a bench. It is a body with a Jack-in-the Box head? You catch my drift?)

Also the First Amendment protections should not allow for a person to be falsely accused or his or her reputation to be fallaciously besmirched. I have been severely victimized by false claims (read about it in my forthcoming biography); such claims can cause unintended and very messy and complicated consequences. (I went to jail when I pulled the trigger based on my assumption that I had a 2nd Amendment right to protect my property and defend my life against imminently approaching harm that was based on a false claim made against me.)

Amendment II is clear in my mind, but the wording does open up the interpretation door. Test it: Can a citizen of the United States freely carry a firearm upon his or her person . . . or not?

I say re-write the Second Amendment. State its intent so clearly and unambiguously so as to not require any opinionated interpretation of any kind and that a child can understand.

And state the 2nd Amendment to exclude the damn licensing requirement. Where did that one come from?

And during the re-writing of the Second Amendment, please clarify the "necessity of a well-regulated Militia" for us. If the 2nd Amendment is so clear and unambiguous, why then are citizens of the United States arrested on the grounds of their involvement with Militias? Or carrying guns?

Also, the Constitutional clause which grants automatic U.S. citizenship to children born to illegal aliens whose first act upon entering our country is a criminal act itself, should be stricken from Amendment XIV.

And while we're at it: Our nation, our Republic, was founded on the principles of the word of God. I say restore those principles and post those words and our commitment to those founding principles on all Federal and state institutions.

Don't like it? Move.

&

Dude . . . tens of millions of our citizens smoke pot.

Marijuana is a natural weed; it is a product of godly nature. I have said for decades that if someone wants to shoot Draino into his or her arms, I ought not be taxed to pay for the "rehab", or an unsuccessful $trillion Drug War, or the whole damn and extremely costly Criminal Justice System associated with a $20.00 "drug bust".

Geez . . . . this is just another insane government policy.

(The American Indians didn't call it "passing the peace pipe" for nothing.)

&

While on the subject of yet another ridiculous government policy: "Support Obesity" . . . with our hard earned tax dollars? Not!

I find it both interesting and disturbing that way too many obese people in America also share a common trait of having tattoos, cell phones and food stamps. Not all . . . but more so than not.

(Related: How can so many of these obese and poor people afford gold teeth?)

&

I would bet that there are an awful lot of people who wish that they had not followed the trend to tattoo their bodies, particularly women and those men and women whose tattoos have faded and have otherwise deteriorated as their skin ages.

I am speaking to you, otherwise unflawed Angelina.

No, I have no tattoos on my body. Don't want any. Well, maybe a small version of a grand piano on my upper left arm . . .

Speaking of which, my friend, renowned artist Leroy Neiman, told me that it is very difficult for him to capture the essence of a grand piano.

&

Memo to January Jones, Snooky, Sophia Vergara and Charlize Theron:

It surely is a blessing to have physical attributes. But Ms. January Jones, your attributes cannot help but paradoxically distract from and enhance your wonderful acting talents. Ms. Jones, and apologies to your husband or boyfriend, I have gazed at you in wonderment.

I have had the pleasure of the company of many beautiful and intelligent women. Ahhh, but you, Sophia Vergara (whose politics and immigration experience is discussed later in this book) . . . exemplify the current wow factor.

Ms. Snookie, you remind me of those little cuties that I grew up with in the streets of Baltimore who defined the original term: Gang banger.

Baltimore, Philadelphia, Jersey City, New York . . . what's the difference?

I compare movie stars of today and yesteryear elsewhere in this booklet. And in that regard, the combination of statuesque beauty and acting talent Oscar has to go to . . . Charlize Theron.

(After seeing "Girl WithThe Dragon Tattoo", I have a secret crush on a different kind of wow-girl, Rooney Mara.)

&

Among the many reasons for the decline of America is what I coin as the Diversity Peter Principle: The hiring and promotion of ill-prepared persons by an organization, business or government on the basis of race, ethnicity, creed, orientation and/or gender is a very fateful practice. And especially so as practiced and mandated by so-called "government standards". And then, adding to the list of harmful government and social practices, there are those most dreaded and oft-times' used and directed deadly terms: Political Correctness (PC) and Racism.

Try providing a proper and sensible education. See how that works.

(See my "Channeling Plan for Education" crafted during my 1998 and 2002 Nevada gubernatorial candidacies. I would say that my Channeling Plan was forward-thinking that very possibly would have yielded a more sensibly and properly-educated American work force to compete in today's international economy.)

&

Question: What is the common denominator characteristic between oil, water and blood?

Answer: They all each coagulate, but not with each other. Which underlines the analogy that no nation can place/ deploy/station or otherwise occupy a sovereign country and *not* be unwelcome.

I argue—and always have argued—that Afghanistan is of little or no strategic global importance to the United States of

America. The exception, of course, exempts the international drug trade.

Aren't the poppy fields beautiful? Ah . . . scarlet flowers and a creamy milky-white sap: sounds inviting, does it not? Well, it is not; it is as deceptive and lethal as any carnivorous flower or plant.

Is there any wonder that the United States, as ordered by the international drug community in order to protect and continue the huge monetary effects of a flourishing underworld and un-taxed economy, overlooks these gorgeous plants?

As I have said for decades, it all comes down to the economics; the money, the hundreds of billions of ultimately American-filtered dollar bills.

And as I have said, including in this tome, "Drug War, my ass."

&

Business, by virtue of its own nature, is ruthless.

Accounting is business's mirror, mirror on the wall.

&

There is no medical doubt in my mind that sneezing activates cold germs.

Proof: What happens immediately after sneezing during the cold season? That's right, first your nose runs and then the other cold symptoms kick in.

Avoid colds: Stifle your sneeze. Squeeze on the tickle spot in your nose (I do, discretely, of course) to prevent colds from spreading in your body. Honestly, it works.

And for Heaven's sake, please cover your mouth when you do sneeze.

&

While I was in jail (for defending my life and property), I struck up a conversation with a fellow inmate who agreed with my theoretical suggestion that water never completely dissipates from the Earth.

During a discussion later on with a neighbor, he added to the theory by saying that the water I consumed today was very possibly drunk by another human, animal or plant centuries, perhaps millions or billions of years ago.

The existence of moisture is the catalyst for that generative process.

It's the old "Bone Song" theory: "Oh, the thighbone's connected to the knee bone; the knee bone's connected to the calf bone; the calf bone's connected to the anklebone; the anklebone's connected" . . . you get the point. Water and moisture go through a similar set of inter-related connections.

Where does moisture come from? Please spare me the scientific makeup of moisture explanation. The question is how is moisture created, which then carry into the atmosphere and morphs into clouds; clouds then become overloaded with large amounts of moisture that create rain; rain pervades throughout all of nature and permeates, sometimes deeply, into the soil from which moisture again rises. ("Them bones, them bones . . .")

Eventually, moisture is re-introduced into the atmosphere in the form of re-generated water. Sort of like Yogi Berra's deju vu philosophy that it all happens all over again. :)

Water never escapes the atmospheric levels of the Earth, so just on that basis alone proves the theory that our old friend, water, has been recycled throughout time and never truly dissipates. Think of the ancient man with whom you now share the glass of water. Hell, we might even be drinking some ancient person.

Another furthermore addition to this theory:

Please note that our human, animal, bird and insect ingestion and release of water, including through plant osmosis, always returns to the Earth and is not ever totally absorbed by, for instance, the physicality of our bodies. In other words, peeing.

Dust-to-dust, ashes-to-ashes. No trace of water. We dry up, but water, including re-cycled pee water, doesn't.

&

The Regeneration/Circular Recycled Water Theory is one point of this particular musing, which brings me to a similar question regarding (my firm belief in) spirituality.

Does spirituality, as I believe does water, somehow regenerate or sort of recycle itself? In the case of humans, does spirituality reproduce itself on the basis of increases in volume (dead people)? Are there lots of little spirits floating around in the Universe awaiting an entire human body donor?

Is that the basis of the re-incarnation theory?

Is the increase in numbers of humans needed to fulfill the continuation of spiritual lives? So, is that why we reproduce? Are there tens of billions of (the spirits of) dead people roaming and squirming around like Petrie dishfuls of sperm bacteria in search of attaching itself (or themselves) to a potential physical life?

Ants don't seem to be bothered by death. Do they know something that we don't know about the eventuality of death?

The answer, in my opinion, is a resounding and unequivocal, and positively and undeniably, and unexplainably-until-actually-experiencing-the-ultimate-experience, YES!

Most people believe that there is only a three-dimensional world. Not I. I believe that there are numerous dimensions in the Universe, including a spiritual dimension and that there is also an entirely separate dimension, which is Life (n.) itself. Do you think of life as belonging in a category of dimensions? I do.

Otherwise, what is it, an entity of some sort?

Life is a dimensional occurrence, a uniquely known and universally accepted 3-dimensional occurrence. The three known and accepted dimensions in life are obviously visible and therefore can be defined in words. But are the range of emotions, such as love and anger, merely by-products of experiencing an emotional life, or do we enter into yet another dimension of life?

And by the way, what is life? Where does life come from? Is there a scientific explanation for life? Is life created though the simple touching of God's index finger as depicted by Michelangelo?

Where does life go after death? Does it go anywhere at all? Life just dissipates? Is there a similar re-cycling process, as it is with water, for life, death, spirituality?

The truth is that we know nothing factual so as to conclusively define the complexities of life. Zero.

Point me not to any form of scripture or writing; rather, bring me forth someone or something that has come back from death to live again.

&

There is another dimension that we could discuss. This one is called fantasy.

Most of us, Westerners in particular, are engaged in supernatural thoughts every day. We call them (fantasy) daydreams. And then at night, we call them dreams. In either scenario, do we not then engage or immerse ourselves into a fantasy world/dimension?

Have you not ever "experienced" a dream? If so, you and I have entered into dimensions that are totally outside of our three-dimensional world that can be successfully argued is no less as real an experience as any during our so-called waking hours. The only difference is tangibility. We can't touch it; nor, conversely, can we touch many of those "real" events that we had experienced mere moments ago.

We interrupt our dream world when we awaken; we interrupt our "real" world by going to sleep. Interesting little twist of life, isn't it?

The Fantasy Dimension could be considered much more of a "real" experience in that one has the ability to immediately recall such an outside of the 3-dimensional experience instead of us trying to peek back into the murky, scrim-framed cloudiness of the nighttime journey that we had just taken though the vision and courtesy of the nighttime dream dimension.

And then, there is the dimension of eroticism. I'll ask my friend, Dr. Laura Henkel to explain that one.

I think that mathematics, science and the arts are inner dimensions that only some of us can bring forward into the light of understanding. Just as in all forms of communications however, not all of us, me included, fully understand such a dimensional world. It's sort of an exclusive club for guys and girls like scientists, Professor Michio Kaku and Dr. L. D. Johnson. But the point is: Are our scientists and mathematicians not reaching into and extrapolating from a separate-from-most-of-us dimension?

By the same token, as do scientists and mathematicians, artists, writers, inventors, etc., do musical composers and performers enter or tap into a separate dimension in addition to our known physical dimensions? Some of them, such as great pianists for example, seem to be absorbed, even controlled, by "another world".

Same question relative to many forms of art or distraction.

Dimensional Exclusivity? Only appointed members need apply? Why is it that seemingly only humans possess "special creative gifts", but not animals?

How about explaining sub-consciousness as being anything other than entering into a dimension?

How about explaining present consciousness as anything other than entering into a dimension?

There are dimensions that we haven't even thought about.

Is imagination a dimension?

&

Heaven and Hell:

I do not believe in the concept of Heaven and Hell.

Instead, I do believe as I have previously stated that upon our death all earthly life and we humans enter into The Spiritual Dimension where new discoveries await us.

Do I sound like "Twilight Zone's Rod Steiger, or "Coast to Coast's George Noory, J. D. Wells, Ian Punnitt or George Knapp?

"Spooky", said Albert Einstein.

If there were such a thing as Heaven and Hell, maybe there would be a form through which we will eventually pass into by death and then ushered through a judgment process, whatever that would or could possibly be. Catholics, for example, believe that there is a sort of court-like Purgatory judgment phase prior to either otherworldly entrance. Given that perhaps it is there and through which such a process that we are evaluated and ruled upon by the Kingdom of Heaven. All of which in total our lives are possibly mitigated on the spiritual level and basis of how we had physically and morally lived our lives.

Regardless of various religious suppositions, I fervently hope that we will eventually be provided the answer to a commonly shared question that we all have pondered: What is the true meaning of life?

Or will it be that we are merely cast or be dissolved away?

Will it be that the physical particles of dust that we eventually become and that basically remain on Earth are somehow once again scattered by the winds of spirituality so as to create new forms, including existing forms of life?

&

Squiggilies.

Keep in mind that we've all come from what I call squiggilies—that's right: a bunch of disorderly, rambunctious little squiggilies running around seemingly incoherently trying to bump into and mate with other squiggilies.

Squiggilies: A new scientific term for those with a decent sense of humor. (Professors Kaku and Johnson: What about this one?)

&

We have vastly underestimated the true age of the Earth. And I believe that it is absolutely impossible to gauge the age of the universe. How are you going to do that accurately? I'd say the number would be close to millions of billions of trillions of zillions of years. Whew!

Explain the true age of just one planet, the Earth for example. Just try to measure how many layers of whatever the Earth consists of.

We haven't got a real clue, do we?

In that context, we must accept that, after all, there is all the time in the Universe to complete its own journey. So what if it takes another couple of billions of zillions of years to fulfill its destiny?

And then what happens?

One thing is certain relative to this discussion: The most important currency that we humans have and that which we would be wise to understand and accept, is that time—that foreign-to-the-Universe concept—is not immortal. So spend it wisely.

&

I have many such deep and curious wonderings, which prompts subsequent and further questioning regarding the true inner-thoughts of many humans throughout recorded history.

As such, and again, I mean not to offend anyone, particularly women of any age by asking the question and then receiving the truthful responses as to whether or not, if they could, would make love to Jesus Christ?

I would then have follow-up questions reserved for another time and place.

&

Cold Fusion:

The next subject that I muse about is the concept of Cold Fusion energy.

There are so many questions that are seemingly as yet unresolved in the scientific community regarding Cold Fusion. But we need a direct and proven answer to the most fundamental of questions in this matter, which is: Watson, does Cold Fusion scientifically exist?

The obvious follow-up questions would have to be based on an answer in the affirmative and then subsequently be proven based on experimental feasibility studies on the subject.

All of us should want to know the answer to the above question, because if Cold Fusion can be proven real, it would cause a tremendous economic impact to the entire world. I am talking about a massive shift in the world's economies and environment as well.

Back to the question: Have the numerous scientific Cold Fusion experiments rendered success or failure in achieving positive energy results?

Were the papers that were written and internationally published on the subject of Cold Fusion by Drs. Fleischmann and Ponds of the University of Utah representative of scientific truth? Is Cold Fusion a viable source of providing energy?

As for my understanding of the question, my answer is absolutely yes.

How do I know if Cold Fusion works despite that I have not conducted my own scientific experiment on the question? First of all, I know what the array of components are involved in conducting the experiment. However, I do not have the scientific laboratory, materials nor the financial luxury (I wish) to conduct such a relatively simple scientific probe. But examples do exist of Cold Fusion tests conducted by well-known and highly respected international scientists. And, reportedly, there are scientists who have claimed to have achieved a positive energy result by re-creating the Fleischmann and Ponds' Cold Fusion experiment.

Therefore, My Dear Reader, if Cold Fusion can be replicated as claimed in numerous experiments conducted around the world, and if Cold Fusion is such a relatively inexpensive energy alternative as also claimed, why are we stuck on oil, which is what I have for decades called the vilest commodity on Earth?

I presume that there must be the same questions on your mind, as well, dear reader.

The quick and easy answer is the same as that which I have applied to everything that affects most, but not all, of our modern world: It all comes down to Economics.

Cold Fusion would absolutely upend the world economy.

And Drs. Fleischmann and Ponds? The last I heard of them, they were living the life of luxury in the south of France.

You, as they say, do the math and figure it out. I've arrived at my own conclusion.

A parenthetical question for my readers: Did you think of Holmes's Watson or IBM's Watson when I opened up this particular discussion by mentioning Watson?

&

The old and now-tired politically-correct double standard:

Nicki Minaj vis a vis Don Imus.

Jackson and Sharpton, as usual, all over it; not a peep from Leslie Moonves or Sumner Redstone . . . except to fire Imus' ass.

&

Trying to quit smoking?

The greatest advice that I received on how to quit smoking and forgive my enemies came from a very wise young man who said, "Don't think about it, Dad".

Thanks, Brucie.

&

Oh come on now . . . surely the Baseball Hall of Fame should admit Pete Rose, who is the definitive example of what a player of the game of baseball is all about, to the Baseball Hall of Fame.

Do it now, without any damn asterisks, and while this guy is still living.

However, there could be a fair warning of admonishment and conditions attached to the Pete Rose admission into the Hall that there shall henceforth be a policy of zero tolerance regarding the behavior of professional athletes, who despite claims to the contrary by some players (Mr. Charles Barkley, are you listening?), are looked upon almost to the point of role-model veneration by sports' fans, particularly youngsters, everywhere.

Wow, can you imagine Pete Rose on steroids? Or Ali? Joe Frazier? O.J.? Tarzan? Arnold? Arnold? . . . Arnold?

&

Answer this one, my fellow Americans:

Which nation in the world has one of the most despicably corrupt, highly taxed, ineptly-managed, war-mongering governments on Earth?

The Answer: The United States of America.

(The above reasons for which I am dedicated to real changes in OUR government.)

&

Separately, but related to the above, in order to provide you with further clarity of understanding of the true and unfiltered Barrack "Barry" Obama, consider that Mr. Obama is rooted in the tradition of another Chicago transplant, renowned poet and avowed Socialist, Carl "Charles" Sandberg.

Make your own judgment on this subject based on the facts, not on the spin. I judge not any man, but I do reserve the right to arrive at my personal conclusions of any and all men. And my presentation of the facts regarding this specific man, Mr. Obama, is based on questioning nothing other than my personal concern regarding the constitutionality, and therefore the legitimacy, of the person controlling the Executive Branch of our government.

&

Related to the race issue, an issue by the way that has long-ago run its course in America, but perpetuated by jerks that prey upon racial-stirring and a racially-guilty-and-sympathetic America with hats in hand:

Ask Oprah Winfrey if she has been stymied in the creation of her immense wealth by racism. Don't ask if she has not been subjected to racism no less or more than I have by "reverse racism", but rather if she has been *prevented* from achieving her success by racism.

What about you, Diddy and Dog? Ice? Damond?

How about you, publishers and producers of "Black" products?

I would say that although it obviously exists on both sides, the thumb of racism in America has lifted.

I think that Reverend King would be pleased—not completely satisfied, but neither am I.

&

As for me: I am going where God takes me.

&

Dear Wal-Mart:

Can you please widen the handles on your plastic bags? I'm having trouble stretching them across my kitchen and bathroom trashcans.

Thank you.

&

I possess no superior intelligence. My relative degree of intelligence is derived from common sense and years of small business experiences, including, as have many others as well, riding the roller coaster of life's successes and failures. That said, I believe that I have the best kind of hands-on business education on account of the importance for a small business owner to know every single aspect of one's business operations from A to Z. I would argue that a hands' on business education is just as educational as attending Wharton or Harvard, whose international business courses I have home-studied.

The basic operating principles of any business are the same whether they are applied to big or small business enterprises.

As a business owner and leader, you have to correctly answer your employee's questions. And for that you need hands-on experience in every aspect of your business. There is no such thing as insight into those types of operational questions. Experience, experience, experience are three of the most important qualifications in running businesses.

For example, I used to wonder why, and despite that I was the owner of my fast food restaurants in Florida, I sometimes had to take out the trash. The answer was soon realized when it became apparent to me that I learned to reduce my trash collection costs by cutting up and stacking the many cardboard boxes thrown away or recycled from my business. Some call that micro-management. For me, it was a hands-on business educational experience that saved me money on operational costs.

As my mentor, Mr. Clifford Perlman taught me, a business leader has to be "The Teller", which is that it is the true and effective leader who clearly defines and instructs an objective, and to know what to do and know how to do it.

I know what to do and I know how to do it.

&

I predict that the next American Revolution will be based almost entirely on what will be politely termed, "philosophic differences". We all know what the true differences are.

Same to same: The World

&

Hey there, you old-timer survivors of the Cold War: Guess what countries are doing comparatively well right now?

That's right, your old evil nemeses, Russia and China.

And you Second World War survivors need no reminder of who our mortal enemies were (Japan and Germany for those of you who attended the current public school system). What a difference a generation or two makes, huh?

And how are the nations of South Vietnam and South Korea doing following those "conflicts" of American military involvement?

Panama? Granada? Daniel Ortega? The Contras? Somalia?

It seems that a proven national growth and recovery strategy and for the financial gains of other nations would be to engage in warfare against the United States.

&

Dead on Arrival:

The wishful idea and original intent that the United States is any more a Republic is dead. DOA.

Sorry, Mr. Benjamin Franklin, we didn't heed your words and therefore just couldn't keep it—a Republic.

&

The China Syndrome:

Revisiting an age-old question: What would happen if we drilled a hole into and then continued on through the center of the Earth? We've thus far barely pierced the outer skin of the Earth. What resources do we now walk upon that have been buried deep inside our planet? Forget the depth to China for a moment; what discoveries await us at only a few miles within the Earth?

What a dig that would be, isn't that so Mr. and Ms. Archeologists?

What is strangely interesting to me from an archeological viewpoint is that it is easier for us humans to explore the outer layers of other planets rather than it is to discover what is beyond the skin of our own planet.

And if ever we were to dig through the entire earth, what would the incredible discoveries be if we then dug through other planets?

And if any of that were to occur, would the end-to-end holes we dig affect the axis stability of not only the planets, but the universe as well?

&

Is it true???

Please tell me that this particular Internet rumor isn't true.

On account of if it is true, boy oh boy, I would sure have some crude things to say—turn your heads ladies and my daughter and granddaughters—about Eight Hundred Million ($800,000,000.00) Dollars of American Taxpayer's money spent to—turn your heads—teach African men how to wash their dicks after having sex.

Quick! Bring in the Myth Busters! "Hey guys, glad you showed up. We've got a little problem even in visualizing this: Can you please demonstrate how and even why the American people are funding . . . ."

I could say it, but I won't . . . I'm sure that you've already said it or at least thought of it, and I'm sure there are at least 1000 jokes out there on this baby. I am one who likes a good joke, so send them on . . . except to say that it is not funny that we are the hard-working American Taxpayer saps that, well, let me say, aren't getting kissed while being screwed.

&

Liberal buzzword: The Community.

&

What gets me is how well Barry Gibbs can continue to sing like that. And how great the brothers still sound, perhaps even better than before the switch from analog to digital recording technologies.

Author's Note: As of the date of this original observation note, August 9, 2011, one of the Gibbs' brothers is very ill. I wish for his recovery. They all appear to me as being pretty good guys.

&

Sharp Dressed Man:

Of all things discussed regarding Abraham Lincoln, there hasn't been relatively too much ado regarding the Lincoln dress fashion.

It was reported that earlier in his years, Abe Lincoln was very proud of his distinctive handsomeness. To prove factual, there is much that one can see in photographs that range from the Lincoln sneer that I interpret as being directed to critics of his facial features, to his body language portraying the confidence of one who is proud of his physical appearance.

Lincoln did dress rather sharply, wouldn't you agree, L. A. Reid?

The top hats, the boots, waistcoats, the sexy dangling ties, the Lincoln posture, the dignity . . . pretty dapper, wouldn't you say, Jay-Z?

How about you experts, Tim Gunn and Carson Kressley, what is your critique of the great one's sartorial style?

&

To L. A. Reid:

What would Simon Cowell know about fashion? Simon has two basic changes of clothing styles, the most common of which is the ever-present and tired-out 70's style of an un-buttoned shirt down to the belly button. (Been there, done that, Simon, but, hint hint, wink wink, that was 40 years ago.)

Now Cowell is exclusively sporting T-shirts with plunging necklines. Grow up, Mr. Cowell.

So now, let's review this abomination called the X-Factor:

In my estimation, Mr. Cowell clearly has lucked out, perhaps played out, in regard to his talent recognition abilities.

The only X-Factor contestant from the last season who has any chance of even having a long-term niche performance success is that 13-year old Glee-type girl who sings and smiles very well and has the potential to expand on such obviously talented gifts.

Conversely, and as everyone is trying to explain to him, that kid Astro's talent is mainly centered on his young age. Know what I'm sayin'? Be thankful for your gift, young man.

I've heard some rap and hip-hop from young artists that would spit his little ass out.

Before we go any further:

I was raised in the mean streets of Baltimore and I made lasting friendships in jail. Most of those dearly cherished friendships are with Jews and black people. Period. Save your labels for someone who gives a good crap about labels.

(The phrase is, Joan Rivers, my old friend from the Caesars' days, a good crap, not a good s_ _t.)

And besides, I had a successful executive position based on my insightful ability to recognize and develop performance talent. So I am imminently qualified to criticize such a waste of time and money as has thus far been the X-Factor.

The entire show is karaoke on steroids.

At the end of the day, as they say on Wall Street, "The Voice" smokes "X-Factor". And the chemistry and talent recognition of the judges on "The Voice" is far superior to all of the other talent shows on television.

To all of the talent shows: Find us another Maria Callas, a Whitney Houston, a Celine Dion, or the soulful musical purity of a Jennifer Hudson or Aretha Franklin. Find us an Adele. And if it is a boy group you are seeking, "II Volo" will give you and us the X-Factor. Please spare us from another screamer. I want people who sing notes, not scream them.

(Side note: I don't know if you would be, but I found it interesting—because somehow I didn't expect it—to hear Aretha Franklin songs played at Frank Sinatra's private house parties. Now there's the number one female pianist/ singer. And yes, I drop the Frank name a couple of times in this booklet.)

None of the X-Factor male vocalists thus far are on the level of Teddy Pendergrast or Brian Mcknight. But there is one young soul singer on "The Voice" who could rise to the top of that category.

Supposedly, the X-Factor super element is that someone is going to blow away an entire national and international audience. Unfortunately, the very model of the X-Factor of people performing and being "discovered" in a karaoke format is simply been-there-done-that, flat-out tired.

The X-Factor talent thus far heard is little more than lounge material, and as such is being elevated—shoved through in some cases—to the next level of competition. (Yes, I was lounge material, which is the reason I didn't cross that fine line either.)

And man, Heaven forbid if the singer doesn't sound "black"; don't even waste the judge's time. (Well, with the possible exception of Brittney.)

The creative fact of the matter, Mr. Cowell, is that on the X-Factor there is no X-Factor.

The X-Factor, Mr. Cowell, if it survives another season, would successfully emerge outstandingly if you were to find a couple of singer/instrumentalist/songwriter/performer/ Pop Stars. Find us a Bob Dylan, a Carole King . . . They are out there. You get the message.

And separately but related: I have been a major Las Vegas hotel/casino entertainment executive, and in that regard, my question is: Oh come on now, does anyone believe that the animal, dance and trapeze acts that typify "America's Got Talent" will regularly pack a Las Vegas showroom?

Howard Stern saved *that* show.

&

Speaking of the Cowell style, we are now seeing the natural progression of drastic changes in men's clothing styles. Starting with the prevalent omission of neckties, business suits are the next style to be eliminated.

We're seeing more Russell Brand individuality than the gray flannel-suited Mad Men.

Let me put it this way: I would not invest in neckties.

In fact, there is little within the brief framework of the past 100 years of both men and women's clothing styles that hasn't changed.

It is, however, interesting in this context to note that throughout practically every historical society the genitalia of both men and women are covered from viewing. Why?

Monkeys have no problem with full exposure.

Women's tops are the next to be eliminated. We're practically there, wouldn't you agree?

&

Ants:

Ants fascinate me. Have you ever seen such unselfish teamwork? Ants are the true survivors of the Earthly eternity. Alas, if only we could communicate with them, what historical tales they could tell.

(How did they survive the Jurassic holocaust? I believe that they merely burrowed several layers underground while other species of Godly creations couldn't. They obviously also had well-stocked storage facilities. And when that ran out, they reacted similarly to humans and other species by resorting to including in their diets, cannibalism.)

Recently, while watching ants building a perfectly shaped mound surrounding their particular nest hole was, for me, a spectacularly interesting sight to behold. Clearly, they must have somehow, somewhere underground manufactured and filtered the distinctively fine sand that eventually surrounded the site.

As for the work ethic, ants are unsurpassed; they literally crawl over each other in a spirit of cooperation that it too is unsurpassed by any species on Earth.

Some ant colonies consist of 12 million inhabitants, and their size, complexities of housing and highway systems compare relatively to New York and London.

Amazing.

The Egyptians, Romans and Greeks must have studied and immeasurably learned from ants' work and social behaviors.

Could any Roman or Greek army have successfully competed with comparably sized African Army Ants? I think not.

I believe that military strategists and hardware technology developers everywhere have learned many things from studying ants. Much is to be learned from ant behavior in many respects.

Respectfully, no suicide bomber, whether Japanese or Middle-Eastern, could compare to the volume and degree of fierce abandon and bravery displayed by all ants. But that's a moot point isn't it, in considering that the consequence always turns out the same: death. So maybe it's a tie.

(BTW: Where does the promise of 21 Heavenly Virgins come from? And what is the reward for the *women* who sacrifice their God-given lives at the alter of Islam? A gaggle of young boys?)

Ants are, next to humans, the most amazing species on Earth. And in my opinion, they will be here long after we have (imminently) blown ourselves up.

Technology is proving itself adept in creating a variety of various forms of life. Little robotic Frankenstein monsters, including some that fly. But while technology cannot capture the life experience due to the element of emotions mixed into the formula, businesses and armies would be well served in emulating ant behavior.

An aside note: A few years ago, some filthy racist Hispanic woman who worked for the DMV in Las Vegas referred to my Japanese wife and our children as "ants". I took it for what it was: some filthy racist Hispanic woman's intended insult, but I also took the slur as a compliment. But I digress . . .

&

Conversely relative to my observations of ants and other insects, I hate flies. What was God possibly thinking when She created flies . . . and those damn mosquitoes?

However, I admire their tenacity. They are persistent and they never give up until either being shooed away, or they lose interest in dumping on your nose or head, or are eliminated.

So, for that reason, but only for that reason, I really admire flies.

And check out termites and hornets.

&

Yes, he's been much aligned as of late, but Prince Harry, or Prince William for that matter, impress me as guys you would not want to mess (cleaned up) with.

I believe that both of them could do the rough and tumble.

&

Taxation:

I believe that a structured national sales tax is the fairest and most equitable form and method of taxation for the United States of America.

More on that later . . .

Meanwhile let's think in terms of what the additional taxation revenues would amount to if every aspect of merely only the drug trade being conducted in America were taxed . . .

&

Generally, the physical effects of the Sun are understood and accepted by most people.

The generally *unknown* factor of the Sun's effect is the psychological element.

Test it:

For many of us, the lack of sun for extended periods of time can psychologically and emotionally be depressing, even causing lethargy. Sunny days, conversely more often do brighten our day. And looking forward to sunny days gives us hope.

The Sun will come out tomorrow . . .

&

Oh yeah . . . returning to Sophia Vergara . . .

Sophia Vergara is a perfect (in more ways than 20) example of why our immigration policy has to now be realistically and sensibly evaluated.

First, a few personal experience facts regarding the immigration process:

1) In addition to my many years of active participation against the criminals who have invaded our county, I have had one of my numerous articles on the subject of Illegal Immigration published by Yale graduate and former Senator Howard Dean classmate, Richard Green. 2) I have been through the excruciatingly lengthy, humiliating and expensive experience with my Japanese (ex) wife when she applied for legal status with the former Immigration and Naturalization Service (INS) to remain in our country, not as a citizen, instead and purely on the basis of obtaining a green card that legitimized her residency in our country.

It is humiliating when armed guards shout down your young children who are packed into a stinky INS (now ICE) service area waiting room for many hours. It was expensive and lengthy for us because we had to hire a lawyer to properly guide us through a ridiculous INS bureaucracy that eventually took years to process.

My wife and our children would have been better served if we had flown from Japan to Mexico City, rented a car, and come over the border illegally just as 30 million Mexicans, South Americans, and presumably Iranians, have done.

By the way, Fumi is a medical professional who could have contributed to our nation.

Furthermore, the assertion that illegals have no "path to citizenship" is a great big lie. I know it; you know it; Liberals know it; the press knows it, etc. etc. So why is it that we hear the same old bull scatology phrases trotted out ad nauseam?

And then . . . we read something like the following statement from an immigrant's point of view: "I am so grateful to be in this country", Ms. Vergara declared in a front-page interview with Parade Magazine.

That is the kind of immigrant in my opinion that our country needs and appreciates. Ms. Vergara has become an amazingly productive member of our society, and speaking on behalf of myself as a citizen of the United States, I am just as grateful to Ms. Vergara as she is to our nation.

Realistically, there are many people in the United States who are, and correctly so, classified as "illegal aliens", but who are also making positive contributions to many of this nation's needs and future.

Don't get me wrong. I stand firmly against any illegal crossing into our country. I say it is a criminal act. And I do not under any circumstances accept that these are people coming into this country doing jobs that "Americans won't take". That is another catch-phrase convenient excuse for the lazy-assed Americans who sit around and collect "government benefits" (or is it "entitlements") at the expense of the American Taxpayer.

In fact, I offered a solution to recently announced work force shortages for farmers, fast-food joints and assorted other businesses in states such as Alabama and Colorado. In that, I suggested that these employers call the Welfare and

Unemployment Assistance agencies in those and surrounding other states requesting that the agencies send able-bodied "government assistance" recipients to <u>earn</u> their living.

Problem solved.

I can tell you that is what I would have enforced if I were the President of the United States.

Getting back to the illegal immigrants, we cannot deny the admirable Latino sense of familia; it is a refreshing change from the fatherless millions in other American communities "fathered" by our taxpayer-funded government. Yes, many of the illegals are calling themselves Americans, and again, courtesy of the American Taxpayer, they are being educated in English and Spanish in most, but not all, of our public schools (another source of my irritation with OUR government).

I suggested in my article published by Mr. Green in 2001 that all persons who are here illegally return to the border that was illegally crossed, pick up an application form to request the granting of an individual's legal status, fill it out, file it and have a copy stamped at our border patrol stations, and then return to either their current residence in the United States or go back to their country of origin. At that point, we will then have "documented" immigrants who will be required within a reasonable period of time to properly file for legal status or citizenship in the United States—just like my wife and one of our sons had to do.

&

Have you ever been to a Welfare office? I have.

During my visits to mostly overflowing welfare offices is that well over 90% of the applicants and recipients in most of the major U. S. markets are either Black or seemingly Third-World Hispanic.

The male applicants, many of whom are strapping and young and therefore capable of working, have the common trait of being decked out wearing at least one or more sports' branded piece of attire.

Other common traits that I observed are that well over 90% of the 90% have cell phones, tattoos, or are either grossly overweight or outright obese.

I found that the women usually apply for government assistance sans (without) the fathers of the babies, and that the majority of those percentages smoke.

Mo' health costs passed on, or more accurately, shoved down the throat of the American Taxpayer.

Do YOU Want The Truth? If so, you just read it.

Read on for more self-evident truths (columnist, Juan Williams, said that there is a "high need for truth in the black community.").

&

Okay, Juan, here's one for you:

"If you take away my Welfare, who gonna' take care of ma' babies?" she asked me, to which I replied, "Try contacting the fathers". "If that doesn't work", I continued, "call Jesse Jackson".

Yes, I have become cynical and have exhausted decades of tolerance in these matters.

As the usually dependable racist slurs and crude (of course) references to my mother were then subsequently heaped upon me, I added, ". . . but don't expect me to pay out another cent for you or yo' babies. I've got my own damn life and set of responsibilities to attend to with zero responsibility to you".

BTW: If I were to become President of the United States, I will have a job for all healthy and able-bodied men and women, which will be the only hand-out distribution form of American taxpayer-funded government assistance.

I made this exact same argument relative to the recent exit of illegal farm workers situation in Alabama and Colorado: Send Welfare recipients to fill those job vacancies.

Oh, I can hear it now: Some racist punk is going to invoke the slavery-in-the-fields metaphor. The truth is that the American taxpayer—black, white, brown, Asian, or pokadot—is the enslaved one, paying out $trillions over generations for the lifestyles of others. That ain't even Socialism. That is, however, no longer acceptable, socially or otherwise.)

Fact: *At least* seventy-two (72%) percent of black babies born in the United States have either been denied or abandoned by the fathers!!!

So don't come down on my white ass with your racist crap for telling it like it is. Fact is that I love and miss the black people that I grew up with in the streets of Baltimore. The disturbing fact is that in the United States of America (!), I cannot walk down those same streets today—in the damn daytime!

Black people are the ones who have to make that change. I remain hopeful for such change, President Obama.

&

The most gorgeous, orderly and polite nation on Earth? Japan. Flat out.

The United States should be number one in that respect, but we have something politely and politically correct, but misnamed, called Urban Communities. Many of these areas of the United States are in reality, filthy, depressing and dangerous. And every one of which is highly racially stressful.

And whose fault is that? We all know the correct answer, but somehow the blame is shifted to others, white people in particular. And we all know who pays the freight charges for the destitution in America. Maybe if we no longer accepted the excuses, we could solve some of the problems.

"Do you think?", as radio talk show host, Heidi Harris questions.

&

In contrast to my above observation regarding the streets of America, Japanese women walk alone throughout darkened neighborhood streets and what we refer to as alleyways at three o'clock in the morning unmolested. Ladies: Try that in America.

If this is the Land of the Free, why is it that I can't walk down the streets of America's cities during daylight hours unmolested?

Nighttime is out of the question.

Land of the Free? Not in much of the United States of America.

Do YOU Want The Truth?

&

Love always feels somehow totally different regardless of how many times we (think we) fall into it.

&

Social Security:

I thank God for Social Security.

For me, Social Security has been a blessing. Social Security benefits provide for me the basic needs for survival. Had it not been forced on me by my government, I most assuredly would not have begun and then sustained payments into the program since I was 15 years old. It isn't that I am disciplined; instead, my life has been on a financial roller coaster to the extent that there have been years during which I could not have faithfully contributed to my retirement financial needs.

The Social Security System is not a Ponzi Scheme, although admittedly it walks, talks and acts like one. It is in fact a forced and tiered government savings investment program for which many of us who are in our retirement years are now grateful to and for.

And the Social Security system is administratively reliable and efficient. I receive my benefits regularly and on time.

It is true that, if computed on a compound interest basis, and on the assumption that we would have invested into another choice of savings' program, the return would be greater than that which we receive from the Social Security Administration.

But, damn it, it has been the crooked politicians who have robbed us of our rightful expectations on our Social Security <u>investments</u>.

Damn thieves. I say set the teaching example: Jail their asses.

African-Americans ought to be ashamed of what your people did to the once mighty, proud and clean Detroit, and Newark, and Oakland, and entirely too many other urban centers ("hoods") in America.

I do not accept the concept of so-called slumlords. Slumlords don't create slums; people create slums.

"Do YOU Want The Truth?—Signature quotation from Bruce Westcott (Or do you want to hear the same old political horse rap from those same thieving politicians?)

&

I am not a racial extremist. I am neither a KKK nor a Black Panther sympathizer. But, damn it (I curse it intentionally and appropriately), I, too often classified disparagingly, am a White Man who is fed up and irritated by the insults and ridicule heaped upon my race.

In fact, anyone who was there will attest that I stood in front of a group of black men while in jail against their reverse racism.

(A shout out to all of my brothers in jail with whom I made quite a few friends. And seriously, mostly all of the guards acted very well towards me while also serving professionally. I think that many with whom I served time would agree with me on both of those points.)

So let's get real.

There are so-called minority groups that claim to have "built this country".

Nonsense *and* bull rap. Do you see hut villages in America? You see the slums, don't you? Well?

Their stupid claim is a misrepresentation of the facts. The fact is that America was built by all of us, but particularly by white Europeans. Conversely, the truth is that America is being systematically dismantled by the few. Unfortunately by those few who are currently in power and who are methodically tearing down the ingenuity, and the brainpower and spirit of our briefly-lived ancestral walls.

Do not be offended by the truth. It is the politically-correct big lie(s) and false assertion(s) that I am offended by and that I wish to correct.

&

It ain't easy being white.

Or being George W. Bush for that matter I guess.

&

I advocate for the political overthrow of this or any other corrupt, poorly managed and wasteful government.

&

Winston Churchill—and he should know based on his vast first-hand experiences with both The Soviet Union and in his own nation of Great Britain—called Socialism "A flop".

&

I don't get it:

How does one go from being a Chicago south-sider or whatever-sider community organizer to then go to work for the government (The People), and within a mere few years spend $50,000 per week—that's $50,000 *per week*!—of "his own money" to numerously rent vacation homes? (Transportation and related expenses not included—courtesy of you and I taxpayers.)

Where did that kind of money come from? How is it factually derived?

How does that happen? Has the person gone into and operated a successful business? Did that person hit the lottery?

How is it possible? Do numbers lie after all?

How does one go about building such wealth within just a few years of working in government positions?

Please provide me the answer Mr. Obama, I want to package it and go on the "Shark Tank" to pitch it for producing infomercials.

Just in case I am misunderstood in this matter, Lyndon B. Johnson is not excluded from this inquiry. I'd love to be able to sound like Jack Kennedy flashing that great smile while admonishing Johnson: "Now you didn't take that a little too far now did you, Lyndon?"

&

Is the assertion really true that President Obama is programmed?

I obviously conclude and respectfully submit that the truthful answer is, yes, Mr. Obama has systematically been politically and religiously indoctrinated since his birth.

The self-documented fact of Mr. Obama's is that there seemingly—in consideration of their political and racially-focused activism—wasn't very much else discussed while young Barrack was sitting on his mommy and daddy's laps and by his mentors, other than religion and politics. The guy has been totally indoctrinated politically and religiously for his entire life. Peri-damn-od.

&

I don't know about you, but I look at life as having only 365/366 days per calendar years that are at its core extremely fluctuating and limited.

There are no guarantees either in or for life. So I try to fulfill my life with varied amounts of joy and happiness; I try to cope with sadness and loss; I am filled with gratitude for the blessing of good health and deal with illnesses.

The rest of my time fulfillment is up to me.

&

It is against all human nature that those who work are forced by government to pay for those who choose to not work.

Again: Slavery is slavery, regardless of how the definition is misstated or misapplied. And if you are enslaved on the basis of money, you are nonetheless enslaved.

&

Fat kills. Prove it to yourself: Tell me when you've ever seen a really old fat person.

And in the context related to this observation, I suggest that soda-blocker Michael Bloomberg take a page from Levittown and create Bloomberg.

Then he could completely rule over his domain autocratically and sans opposition.

&

I think that in 1998 I possibly conducted one of the first Internet-based gubernatorial candidacies in our nation.

A plank in my Education First and Foremost platform was my Channeling Plan for Education, which included a proposal to install computers in all kindergarten and first-grade classes. I suggested that as both of the lower grades progressed, the kids would take their computers with them throughout their elementary education years. The computer placements would be repeated with every subsequently new kindergarten and first grade classes so as to soften the all-at-once costs of providing entire systems to all grade classes. It would be a phased-in process.

(Based on my research, I believe that at the time Nevada would have benefitted through contributions from computer companies, including Apple and Microsoft.)

One woman stood up at one of the Meet the Candidates' forums that I participated in and called me a Nazi for proffering such a disgusting proposal.

No wonder I didn't win. Look at the mindset that *I* had to overcome. Forget that the election was instead an anointment process for the eventual winner (read author, Jon Ralston).

You've surely seen and heard enough of today's phony-baloney that is passed off as "news", but while I am on the subject of my political candidacies, there is a point that I would like to make relative to the news and media, particularly in Nevada, that I experienced. Worst of all that I can tell you on this subject is that the following example pervades throughout Media America.

It all boils down to something referred to in polite circles as the writers "influencing" their readers. In wartime Germany and in Communist propaganda literature, it is referred to as "brainwashing". In the United States of America, it *is* brainwashing.

Steve Sebelius is the Las Vegas Review Journal's top political communist . . . eh, columnist.

In 2002, in addition to myself and others, there was a seasoned politician named Joe Neal running for Governor of Nevada. Joe was a good old guy, albeit not one of the good old boys—you see, Joe Neal was a black man.

Parenthetically, Joe Neal was a friend of mine. But Joe and I were polar opposites politically. Joe gave me a ride home one afternoon following a funeral for a mutual friend of ours during which Joe and I had a private debate regarding our political differences. Joe didn't sway me; I didn't sway Joe.

So Steve Sebelius called me one day for a newspaper interview, which led to a real-time exchange of e-mails, and during one of which Mr. Sebelius offered me the following (paraphrased) question: "Don't you, deep in your heart, believe that Joe Neal would be the best choice for our state's governor?"

"No", I replied, "but Steve, what gives you your obvious reason to think so?"

Steve Sebelius responded, "Well, he wants to raise taxes on gaming in Nevada." (The Nevada casino owners loved that one.)

I replied, "Steve, name one other issue, matter or program other than raising taxes on gaming that Mr. Neil advocates for in his candidacy?"

Silence. He was stumped.

That concluded the interview.

This "Thumb Sucker"—my opinionated term for this arrogant jerk, is the Las Vegas Review Journal's top political Marxist Democrat . . . eh, columnist.

Admittedly, over these subsequent years, bowling ball head has improved in his writing. I guess that being married to a successful attorney can raise one's I.Q. But the episode points out that the very important issue of The Media Matter in America is that although these people don't know their asses from a hole in the ground, they nevertheless and nonetheless brainwash/aka "influence" the masses.

"The Media Brainwashing of America"—my title, you write the book and send me royalties.

&

Your reputation is often based on what others think and say about you. But they haven't taken your opinion of what you think of yourself into neither consideration nor the equation.

For some, you are the one who has to take some consideration into account of your own equation conclusion. Or, as Brother Al would say, treat it like sex. (You'll have to figure that out.)

Gore Vidal says that it matters not what others think of you; it matters only what you think of them.

&

Shadows:

We take our shadow(s) for granted.

An interesting diversion in viewing one's self is to look at one's various shadows.

Try it. Analyze it. Start making your physical corrections based on what you see in your shadow as well as what you view of yourself in your mirror.

Try to see your physical and character self as others might see you from the perspective of your shadow.

In some ways, looking and analyzing your shadow is, if not sometimes a better view of yourself then through a looking glass. It is at least a different viewing perspective for you to contemplate of your physical self.

A shadow is not necessary a spitting image of yourself, but it is an image of you nevertheless, and even mirror images are not always true. Sometimes elongated, sometimes distorted, sometimes brutally honest, a shadow is nonetheless somewhat of an image not unlike what passer-byes fleetingly or glancingly see of you.

Get yourself in the right light, both literally and figuratively. Then review your shadow.

By the way, your shadow follows you everywhere. "It isn't paranoia if they really are out to get you." You know?

I am fascinated by shadows and clouds.

&

Don't worry. Be happy. The world is just about ready to blow itself up.

&

If you think, as I do, that the Arab Spring is potentially internationally dangerous, take a deeper look in knowing that the world is vulnerable to a united Muslim/Islamic uprising.

Is the imminent clash of religions (Judeo-Christians versus Muslims) the basis of the Armageddon? Or will the World Economy be the catalyst? Also, I can easily visualize a divisive racial war under easily-predictable conditions.

I think that the next and possibly final big one will be based on religious differences.

Scary factoid: All three possibilities, it must be pointed out, are in play in this very present day scenario.

It conceivably could be noted that in the future—by whom, I do not know who's going to be around in the future—that religion killed the world.

If that or any of the other prevailing world conditions continue unresolved, it could be that we humans are merely hanging around and existing during this planet's imminent demise.

Reminding you of ants . . .

&

The problem with our frigging government is that it is upside down. It's supposed to be bottom-up, not trickle-down.

And we as a nation are on such a frigging obviously wrongful course. How much longer am I, or are you, going to have to say this before the rest of our citizens—I mean <u>all</u> of our citizens—see it?

Ah, duh? W-e a-r-e a-l-l i-n t-h-i-s b-o-a-t t-o-g-e-t-h-e-r.

&

Pointing out a few examples of empires contained in history's trash bin:

The Inca Empire

The Roman Empire

The Egyptian Empire

The Alexander and Greek Empires

The Persian Empire

Great Britain

The Queen Victoria Empire

The Harappan Empire

The Morian Empire

The Soviet Union

The United States of America

Catch my drift?

P.S. Do all civilizations eventually fall into ruin? If so, why, and is there a common thread or cause; and if that is the case, what is it and is "it" now irreversibly imbedded into the fabric of the United States of America?

Now there's a political issue for you to discuss.

&

Speaking of empires . . . To the Greeks of whom it is written are a people of glory and valor; who are arrogant and headstrong and highly evolved; to the Greeks, who represent the term and creation cradle of Democracy, and who have laid the groundwork and contributed so much to civilization itself; to those of you who walk the same lands and fish the same waters as did the great philosophers and architects before you; to those of you who are genealogically derived from those who ruled during perhaps some of the most extraordinary periods in human history, and you, who have accomplished sooo much more:

HOW COULD YOU? . . . have accepted such a foolish and un-natural economic doctrine as that of Socialism?

&

Socialism is against half of all human nature.

&

In a Capitalist society, jobs are the fish that feed.

It is possible that capitalism was originated in parts of the world where you can't fish.

&

What is it that would reconcile the arrogance of mankind that thinks the evolution of humans and nature, if there is such a thing, is now complete?

If we live that long—I don't believe that we will, but if we do, I believe it is possible that humans will evolve to the extent of not having any use for hands and feet.

Humans will control their lives highly efficiently and effectively through mind and gadget controls that will be instructed by human telepathy brainpower (there's that prediction again).

That's right. Look mom, no hands . . . and feet and arms and legs. Just a head sitting on top of a minimum of body encasement containing organs efficiently arranged and necessary-for-life's-normal and abnormal functions.

We can see that vision right now: Google Stephen Hawkings or look at the envisioned odyssey of Hal, the futuristic computer. Hal has no organs per se—and no emotions. And Hal and other evolving scientific and engine technology require only a renewable power source, so there's no waste.

And Hal is old news.

So, what's ahead for the human race, if we exist that long, in another trillion years?

Just a head . . .

&

It is a matter of our national interest to insure that America lives up to its promises of providing reasonably unbridled libertarian freedoms. I am not a Libertarian—not that it's all bad or good. Currently, I am affiliated with the Reform Party of Nevada and I recognize David Collision as Chairman of the national Reform Party. However, I have been an independent candidate for President of the United States and as such have proffered an entrepreneurial plan to provide all Americans with opportunities and jobs of all sorts at decent living wages. I can also ensure that, as President, America will fully participate in providing good science and technology while assuring environmentally sensible and pure water and air to its citizens.

If we are to lead the world by example, we have got to rein in the environmental damage to our planet. And the best way to do that is to turn the oil economy into a green economy. We need a sensible phasing plan for such a change. So, on that point, I do agree with the Obama administration. With my plan, no one loses a job. Instead, we will create incredible amounts of new and good-paying (". . . enough to go to a movie and buy a Hershey Bar"—B. W. 1998) jobs, jobs, jobs.

In many cases, it is going to take a couple of decades to make all of the conversion/transition/restructuring of America. However, there are some of our problems that merely require quick and sensible leadership-level solutions. The good news is that we can do it because we know how to do it. America has the brainpower and the technology. And it would possibly surprise you if I told you where a golden amount of that brain matter exists.

Oh, to Hell with it, I'm gonna' say it: Incarcerated black guys kick ass in the game of Chess, which to my observation proves their level of intelligence. And one of the reasons why they are such excellent chess players is that they (usually) can't cloud their brains with drugs while incarcerated in jails and prisons. So imagine if all of that brainpower were unleashed sans under the influence of drugs . . .

This observation tells me that these guys would generally be great in many things related to computers.

Test it: First, exclude those severe-crime offenders; they must rightfully be punished. Then apply my Channeling system to those other offenders of punk-ass crimes that would determine individual aptitudes and interests in all areas of computer technology. In a word(s): Provide Opportunities. And start the training in jail.

Wouldn't it make better sense to produce tradesmen instead of bureaucrats and prisoners?

Damn it, I'll say it over and over if I have to in reminding our citizens that these are not Democrat and/or Republican issues. The truth is that in too many respects these are survival-as-a-nation issues. The United States of America is a poorly-steered ship at sea right now.

&

As possibly the best-ever interviewer in broadcasting history, aren't there times when you want to shout out to Charlie Rose to please shut up and listen to his guest's answers?

I know that here are times when an interviewer rightfully interrupts a guest to explain a particular situation to viewers and listeners or to keep a guest in context to the subject matter, but methinks that Mr. Rose doeth interrupt a wee bit too often.

Other than that, Charlie Rose, as is Don Imus when he is not being insulting, a superior broadcast interviewer.

&

Since spending, or more correctly stated, pissing away, hundreds of billions of dollars, perhaps a trillion dollars ($1,000,000,000,000.00) over the long haul, on an absurd and mismanaged "Drug War", including the failed appointments of Drug Czars, criminal prosecutions, costly incarcerations, and assorted other related costs, guess what? The whole thing has been a huge failure.

Need I really say more? Well, I will, I have, and I will continue to rail against such senseless government waste.

One way would be for us to spend that money on remedial education programs for those black brains now rotting in (expensive) jails and prisons.

Do YOU Want The Truth?

&

Even Theodore Roosevelt wanted to simultaneously be President and control Congress.

"Reform is the antidote to revolution"—"Teddy" Roosevelt.

"Nothing gets done by committee"—Fisher Pen founder (and a fellow Kentucky Colonel), Paul Fisher

Q: Can any politician named Teddy have the slightest chance of being elected today? Discuss . . .

(Michael Savage's dog, Teddy, is disqualified relative to this discussion on the basis of intellectual osmosis.)

&

Attention: My Fellow Americans:

Government is essentially defined as being an entity that provides services and protections to its national citizens. However, Americans are failed by our government in not receiving internal protection services.

In order to correct this glaring disparity, we need to bring our military home to provide internal protections and services to all of America's communities and businesses.

As I pointed out earlier, why is it that I, a citizen of the United States of America, cannot drive through, nor walk on the sidewalks of certain neighborhoods in our own cities?

If we are to be a nation Of, For and By our citizens, don't you think that we should be a united nation?

&

America First and Foremost!

&

I am The Messenger—Bruce Westcott

&

The logic of withdrawing and redeployment from the Middle East:

I start this condensed essay by repeatedly pointing out one very specific and underlining principle of fact, which is that no nation can place/deploy/station its military into a sovereign country and <u>not</u> be unwelcome. Ask any social psychologist.

An exception in our case would of course be that we would thoughtfully consider requests from other nations for us to station or maintain a relative-to-needed U. S. military presence within their sovereign boundaries. The various parts of our decisions on such a matter would be weighed heavily in consideration of humanitarian appeals, and would range to questioning the logic of such deployment relative to our own national strategic interests.

My plan is to maintain our entire military personnel in its full and complete entirety. However, I am persuaded that we need only four or possibly five *regional* military presences globally.

Our military personnel represent a highly trained and proven-competent workforce. And they are armed and ready to defend our nation. We, therefore as citizens of this great nation, recognize the need for every single military person that we have, including those who, through their experience and those whom we can and will assist through training, can make significant contributions to many of the internal challenges that we as a nation have at hand.

We have much for our military to do in the dual-roles of protecting us from our enemies, thereby securing us as a nation, and through contributing to the enforcement of the current laws of our nation. If it were to become a Westcott administration, our military shall continue to act as our nation's protectors and shall be given every tool, benefit and honor that is deserved for its service to our nation.

And . . . for the most part, our military personnel will be stationed at home. (I believe in the "range weaponry" theory (proved by the advent of the long bow) mixed with the "boot" requirement in wartime.)

We have a border problem in our nation that I'd like to have realistically investigated by our military planners and be given recommendations on how to solve protecting our borders, all four of them.

&

From the "Great American Hot Dog & Draught Beer Emporium" (an actual Bruce Westcott entrepreneurial creation) to the "Great American Wall":

If I were to become President, I would request that our military planners assign a logistical team of engineers, designers and estimators to provide my office with a comprehensive study for constructing the "Great American Wall" across our entire southern border with our neighboring nation and the fine peoples of Mexico.

I want the Great American Wall to be the most defining and profitable six/eight/ten lane highway system—and attraction—in the world, including aqueducts, bridges, walkways, bicycle and scooter paths, guard houses and retail quick stops along the way. Entrance fees and tolls will apply—a self-sustaining economic concept.

I trust that our citizens who have property along the wall's route will cooperate with the rest of us on behalf of the better good of our nation by subordinating slices of border property to this important project for our nation's protection and economy. The current owners will have fair exchange options in return for their contributions to our nation.

Our entire nation needs rebuilding. We *can* afford the costs because everything that we do for our nation in rebuilding our nation, we shall do with American products, services and personnel. Jobs, American jobs filled by Americans. Millions of Americans.

We will create an economy that provides sufficient operating capital to our government while helping to pay down our (renegotiated) debt

Some of what we do in regard to these massive construction projects will be based on the valuable expertise and experience of our military; some from private enterprise; all of which will be exemplified and defined as being the American Spirit and Know-how, the ingenuity of her people, and as The Great American Wall becoming among America's newest and shining modern achievements.

I don't know about you, but I get sick in seeing the deterioration and blight and disrepair in this country.

The economy of the United States of America, starting with that one or two, albeit major, adjustments in our present spending, will insure that we—all of us—shall begin to enjoy a very robust way of life that we possibly have merely misplaced for the past many years.

I'm no Certified Public Accountant, but I did study college-level Principles of Accounting courses, and I do have extensive and valuable small-business experience. My calls have been taken respectfully and respectively from several Wall Street leaders. I know how to transfer costs and revenues from column A to column B. I can assure Americans that there will be no need to increase our taxation revenues from working Americans simply because we will transfer costs from one accounting column to another column, and do the necessary-to-a-robust-economy-and-efficient-government trimming from there.

Through my leadership, we shall bring the vast portion of our men and women of the military home, and transfer those costs of rebuilding other nations to the rebuilding of America.

The fact is that, as I said—excuse me, but I think it important to stress the importance of a sensible Foreign Policy—in today's technological world, we need only four or five international military bases strategically placed throughout the world.

And, as Commander-in-Chief, I will assure our friends and foes that the United States of America will not conduct one-arm-tied-behind-our-backs, patty-cake wars.

I hop upon no wagon. I've been preaching the above for decades.

The Great American Wall will be a profitable venture and international attraction for America instead of "investments" in corporate failure and greed.

And then we will study the long-term economics of building a waterways' system in America. Such a plan could easily be accomplished by merely constructing a water distribution system along and parallel with our current and future highway systems.

And then there are the Prudhoe Bay gas reserves . . .

The Keystone Project is a great and practical idea. We just have to—no more studies, we've enough—implement that nationally important concept carefully.

(See that? We've conceivably generated a new addition of friendship and prosperity to our regional solidarity neighbors. And that includes Mexico. I love Mexicans—not all, but I have some beautiful and remarkable Mexican-descended neighbors and friends throughout many areas of our nation.)

&

Here is another Presidential Accounting Adjustment from Column A to Column B:

All financial aid to countries such as Israel and Egypt, and Somalia and The Sudan, et al. shall henceforth be stopped. We will use those $tens of billions per year on something useful and productive to America.

I know that there are enough Jewish and Egyptian supporters in the world who can provide the nations of

Israel and Egypt with an equal amount of the $billions each per year now being provided by the American taxpayer (unconstitutionally BTW) to those nations. And certainly as well, the (substantial) new money in the black international community can financially match the assistance to African nations (again: unconstitutionally) now being also provided for by otherwise unwilling American taxpayers.

A nation's charity begins at home. In the case of the United States of America, international charity and our Foreign Policy are Constitutional issues. If we're speaking of an individual's placement of a charitable contribution, that is an entirely different individual prerogative.

(Think of the world if those $billions contributed to negative political ads were to be diverted to nations in need.)

However, let no nation mistake that all nations with whom we are allied we shall honor our commitment to defensively lock arm and arm with throughout the world.

And while we are touching on the subject of Foreign Policy, the United States shall also withdraw from the United Nations.

The United Nations building in New York could be converted into a profitable asset for the United States' balance sheet.

Want another fact? The U. N. is (other than local politicians, who are excluded in this matter on the basis of sameness) the deepest of well sources for prostitution in New York City.

There are several very positive windfall economic benefits to the United States in making these types of simple accounting adjustments. It's part of "The Formula of Sensible Ideas and Solutions" (see brucewestcott.org).

&

I am armed. I have a pen.

&

Man, this writing thing is a workout.

&

Who dat? . . . who dat? . . . who dat who say who dat when I say who dat?—An old Baltimore Street (there is such a street in Baltimore) playful funny.

&

Switching speeds metaphorically . . .

Author's Note: The following can be proven to have been conceived of prior to recent scientific challenges to Einstein's Theory of the Speed of Light:

To answer a question previously hypothesized within this book: Time is faster on the basis that the speed of light is not accurately calculated.

The correct speed of light formula is encapsulated by the following non-professional description:

LDTDD = ACLRTT:

L: Light, as within the context of current human understanding + D: Dissipation of light as it travels must be considered in any accurate calculation of the Light Theory + T: Travel + D: Distance + D: "Dust" = The Accurate Calculation of Light Relative to the Travel of Time.

Note: Admittedly, my non-professionally designed formula requires a classic scientific explanation.

Meanwhile, for purposes of inciting thought on this subject: Factually, we now know that there exists a universal field of an unexplainable "dust", possibly in the form of as yet undiscovered matter or particles of some sort (relatively recently-discovered neutrinos, for example) that light must pass through, and therefore which must be taken into consideration within any accurate scientific projection or equation when calculating light relative to, or versus, time travel.

Ask any Quantum Mechanics' scientist if the mysterious "matter" has yet been discovered on which, or through which, objects, including planets, can conceivably make Quantum Leaps. The answer is that such a mystery has not been either solved or even discovered. But, most assuredly, there has got to be *something* that exists between those suspended rotating spaces that allows for Quantum Leaps.

For purposes of exploring an example: The scientific community now agrees that neutrinos exist in the universe. Right? Couldn't there be an equally reasonable assumption that massive amounts of neutrinos, for example, constitute a field of resistance, however minor, to the calculation of time travel? Does that factor of resistance not deserve consideration within the present scientific calculations of both light and travel?

Respectfully, E=MC2 no longer gets it for me. I'd like to be further convinced on the basis of questioning if there is an unknown element not included in Einstein's equation.

In explaining the (unknown) dust theory relative to this projection, if it is not specifically neutrinos, there is most assuredly *something* that exists in the air (or matter) of space that needs to be taken into consideration when attempting to correctly interject and therefore calculate any degree of resistance or delay that is present in both light measurement and that through which space travel must or can be navigated.

Perhaps that "something" is gravity. How about the yin and yang theory relative to gravity that in these pages questions if there is an opposite force on the other side of gravity. Can you see gravity? Can you see the neutrinos that are now scientifically-measurably proven to be passing through our entire being and all such related matter existing in the Universe?

Whatever it is, the existence of a resistance field or factor must unquestionably be included in any accurate calculation through which light is projected to travel, and therefore through which would alter, however slightly, the currently-accepted light and curvature of time travel projections and formulas, IMHBEO—In-my-humble, briefly-educated-opinion.

My own revelation of this theory came to me @ 2:00 am on 2/05/2011 during which I could see the light of a flashlight continuing to linger in the dark *after* I had shut off the flashlight. That experiment alone proved to me, at least or got me thinking, that light is not as instantaneous, nor does light dissipate as previously believed in past and current scientific measurements.

The travel of the light that I witnessed was slowed down by some sort of a scrim composed of various particles, matter, or "dust", and through which we haven't as yet broken through scientifically or technologically.

Maybe we ought to be more considerate of possibly wrongful basic scientific assumptions in crafting our (therefore possibly wrongful) equations.

Perhaps there is that something yet-unbroken-through field of resistance type of element in my amateur calculations that could be overcome, or mystery solved, that will provide accurate answers to even the basic possibility of time and space travel questions.

Are there other sets of (obviously undiscovered) physics in this or any other universe? What? Are we that pompous or perpetuating Stone Age ignorance to think that there cannot be other physics?

I can tell you what a B-flat 13th chord is . . . but I leave it to the scientific mind to devise a mathematical formula to more concisely explain or disprove the above theory.

&

Women are vastly more discourteous drivers than men.

No need to construct a formula to prove or disprove that fact. (I can feel the glares . . . :)

&

Professor Stephen Hawkins says that there is no God.

Professor Michio Kaku says that there has to be God.

I think that most people believe in a godly spiritual dimension to or through which we humans must evolve by death in order to ever discover either truth.

My own experience has been that I have, unquestionably in my mind, been contacted by my recently departed family both in dreams and through spiritually-conveyed numerology. I believe that I have been allowed and able to enter into a spiritual dimension connection to my ancestors.

No, I do not engage in any sort of verbal intercourse with my spirits and angels.

Hey, some people do claim to have an actual conversation with God. Not I. But I am contacted spiritually . . .

&

Adam and Eve would have to have had an incestuous relationship following their creation of being.

Think about it: How else could there have been a subsequent lineage?

Adam would either have had a sexual relationship with his daughter, or a son and a daughter would have had to have been born and they, or either of their parents, in turn, would have had a sexual relationship.

There is no reference that I know of to any of the above theory in The Bible.

Surely however and according to Christianity, at first there were two people, Adam and Eve. At that point, God let us take over the reproduction duties and responsibility and from that there was conceived a third person. Then a fourth. And from that point forward we are all derived and therefore, according to the Bible and this theory, we are all brothers and sisters.

Hello, please to meet you, my brothers and sisters. Hijimemashite, as they say in Japan.

All of the above serves to prove the theory that we are all related throughout the time during which we humans have occupied the Earth. But what about other species of life? Animals, for instance, if there ever had been such a thing as an Adam and Eve of animals and any or all species ever represented on Earth.

Is there a Heaven and Hell for animals? Insects?

See my comments on Ants. They know something about immortality that we human mortals obviously cannot even comprehend.

BTW: The Bible has no similar or related references to animal heaven, nor for insects. Ah, but getting back to dogs and cats, and pets in general, we think of them passing into heaven.

&

Relative to the reproduction process, why does it feel so good?

It is interesting to me that during having sex with others or through masturbation a person can simultaneously experience the varied senses of sublimity, fantasy, and real physicality.

Through what other form of activity can that combination of effects be achieved?

Weird isn't it that our physicality reacts to the cravings of the mind? And that once the physical aspect of our sexual cravings climaxes, the mind is satisfied as well.

Do the mind and the physical go off into separate dimensions during having sex?

Doesn't one overrule the other?

Just asking and saying . . .

&

Diversity killed Alexander the Great.

Integration of Persians and the introduction of other unwilling conscripts into the Alexander the Great army battalions that had originally consisted of rank and file and highly nationalistic Greek warriors, proved to be a disastrous, albeit understandably necessary, Alexander decision.

&

"Off with their penises!", shout the women.

Well girls, good luck humping each other for as much as a generation, but you, those of you who shout your slogans, won't be around either.

Which proves the point that men are here merely to serve women. Right?

Okay, yes, I did forget to consider the frozen sperm technology in the above paragraph. "Kid on a stick", as my friend, comedian Lonnie Shorr, said during his great performances.

&

Did you, or do you, think that youth would last forever?

&

Me and my computer. Oh where would I be without thee?

Thy too my cellithphoneth. And thy too, all of the other contraptions of our Age of Technology.

I have an ongoing love/hate relationship with modern technology. (Please see, "Ain't Technology Grand?")

&

Please someone: provide me with an answer as to why no one during the time of Jesus on Earth neither foresaw, predicted, wrote or spoke of, or otherwise knew of the North And South American continents. Or the North and South Poles? Or the South Pacific, or the North Atlantic and other mighty oceans? Or the continent of Australia? Or the Island of Japan?

I think this is a valid question.

&

Isn't it interesting that there are certain periods in history during which there seem to have been a surge or births of groups of individuals that have provided our species with various categories of significant intellectual, scientific and artistic development and contributions?

And that often these individuals existed within the confines of certain geographical boundaries.

For example: From Central and Eastern Europe came the great musical composers. (Can't count Chopin as a Western European despite his fondness for living in France, his cut-out heart went to Poland.)

The Renaissance. The Greek philosophers. Italian artists. Spanish artists, French artists. Modern technology in America. Jazz in America. All of which seemingly arose within a certain period of time or geographical location. Referred to here as the Phenomenons Within the Various Ages of Mankind.

Granted that there is not necessarily an exclusivity factor in grouping or categorizing the above phenomena, but it does seem to me that much of what is described above had either a common occurrence, convergence, and/or emergence relative to time and geography. Or there could possibly be an explanation attributed to the religious and/or political climates of the day, in which case I favor the religious explanation to which I cite the Medici patronage period.

And, of course, there are those who attribute past and present genius to ET's.

&

An age-old question: What did Jesus look like?

Even the great DaVinci could not have accurately captured Jesus' countenance. Nor did Michelangelo.

Why is it that so much had been written during only His later years and after the life of Jesus on earth that there was, nor is, no artist's true depiction of Jesus?

People didn't draw or paint any images of Jesus? The Sermon on the Mount or the real Last Supper was not captured by any artist or even by a simple commoner, a waiter, or accomplished artist during a time in which the Roman Empire contributed to a prolific plethora of historic art production?

Was there a ban on depicting the image of Jesus? If there were authentic image depictions of Jesus, were they all outlawed, then burned or buried, or could they have been hidden in such a way so as to (hopefully) be discovered on another day?

Wouldn't it have been customary of the day to have included artifacts, or articles of clothing or belongings, or some sort of drawing or painting of the image of Jesus in His tomb? A piece of pottery? Shoes? A burial shroud?

How can we say that the famous Shroud is an accurate depiction of Jesus? What would be the comparison image? Truth is, we can't. We can hope, speculate, theorize and so on, but proof . . .?

I think that someday there will be an archeological discovery of artistic renderings of the true image of Jesus. I pray for it. It will be such an uplifting experience.

Perhaps one of those Middle East bombs will uncover and therefore expose that secret.

Wouldn't it be great to see the accurate and true image of God? I remain hopeful.

&

As we continue our exploration and discovery throughout the universe, one of the great things about modern technology is that it provides for us the understanding and proof that many things that we previously dared not envision—to many, what was the point?—are indeed possible.

We can now see the much of the future. We can accurately predict numerous things that will actually *occur* relative to man's abilities to achieve the previously unthinkable.

For example, think of what we did or did not scientifically know or understand a mere couple of hundred years ago. Would we have then known unequivocally that space travel, and so much else in any of the sciences, was actually possible?

Buck Rogers showed us that we could space travel. (Weren't those Pop Art drawings an amazing set of futuristic blueprints? Are you listening Mr. Spielberg? . . . Mr. Lucas?)

And now, amazingly, we *can* see the future—at least the immediate future. We no longer have to wonder if we will ever travel to the Moon or Mars. We can; we know that we can, on account of we have.

Another great thing from a historical perspective is that we are filming and recording practically everything that is going on in the world today. Imagine if we had this technology during the Greek and Roman Empires' eras; the construction of the pyramids, both Great and Aztec; the Crucifixion . . .

It is amazing how far we have come in a relatively amazingly short period of documented history. We are in an as-yet-accurately-labeled age of history. And at least half of us don't realize it.

Unfortunately, unless we in the world get our mound of dirt together in the context discussion of seeing the future, I doubt that we eventually are *not* going to blow ourselves up. In fact, it's highly unlikely that *won't* happen. I only question as to why, if we are so smart and if we can see the future, that we cannot see such an imminent occurrence as the (Biblically predicted) Armageddon. ???

&

There is an old question that asks who you would choose from history to have dinner with.

Ordinarily, the names Jesus Christ and Hitler come up during such a discussion.

On a little more minor note: I would like to film at least four hours with the following four guys sitting at a table and milling around on a ranch together:

Willie Nelson, Don Imus, Kinky Friedman, and Billy Bob Thornton.

I invite you to send me your modern-day foursome (for discussion . . .) choices.

&

The China Effect on the World:

What's there to figure out? If you give one billion-plus people, particularly homogenous people with brains and an economic incentive, there is bound to be an astounding economic and financial result.

In China, and taking into consideration the above paragraph of this observation, by entrusting the objective of creating both individual and collective growth and development in the fields of manufacturing, science, technology and an economy-fueled military might courtesy of Wal-Mart, the eventuality of the rise of China as a dominant world power, both economically and militarily* could have easily have been foreseen.

*The world concerns itself with a million-man Chinese army. Well, the reality is that it would be not be at all impossible for China to mount a 100+million person army.

Then what would be the military outcome of that unfortunately easily conceivable scenario? What about a 200 or 500-million army poised toward an enemy of China?

(Another parenthetical: During only as recently as during the past century, how did Japan conquer China prior to the Japanese being bullied out of China by the Russians? Answer: Technology and organization.)

However, the brutal fact of today is that the only defense against such a formidable army is to implement the nuclear option.

Personally and frankly, I have rued the day of the Nixon/ Kissinger "China Initiative" that awakened the sleeping giant nation of China.

It's too late now.

Mr. Kissinger, I do understand the international chessboard strategy of your China policy vis a vis the (former) Soviet Union. But look at the resultant Chinese tiger that arose, Sir.

Did we merely substitute one significant national enemy (the Soviet Union), with another (China)? I think so.

And now we have the additional worry of a conceivable religious war upon us.

What about the smaller conflict testing grounds? ("Conflict"? Tell that to our nation's veterans and dead of those misnamed wars.)

In this regard, are America's enemies intentionally perceived? Isn't there a hunger metaphoric factor (see my Universe theory) created by Eisenhower's insightfully perceived Industrial and Military Complex warning? Do we—and the world—need to have enemies to feed the I&MC economic appetite?

I think so. It falls under the (Accounting) category of Manufacturing and Employment. You economists know what I'm talking about.

As of the date on my notes of this particular observation, 2/18/2011, China is realistically the world's largest economy, albeit restrained or even reigned-in by its governmental directives and some foreign pressure (the U. S. and Japan), but with no turning back foreseen—unless by war.

So I guess that we're just going to have to have a damn war.

China has merely to mature from these early stages of childhood-like development to an imminent and unrestricted-by-outside-forces transition to adulthood. At that point is when the China Effect on the world will really kick in.

&

And on further thought, if we did drill that hole through to China, wouldn't that affect the entire Universe more than just tipping the Earth's axis?

Fly me to the moon . . .

&

I love trees.

I love riding a well-oiled, properly inflated bicycle.

I love a rainy night and candlelight.

I dearly love my children.

Who or what do you love?

Q: Do you love PBS's Mr. Rogers? A: (Spoken in Mr. Rogers' soft and polite tone) I do now.

&

Weren't the movie stars of yesteryear more beautiful and elegant than today?

I'm not talking about bodies. Today's bodies are much more superior, although most of us can't tell what is real and what is, shall we say, inauthentic. I'm talking about those faces of yesteryear's movie crop and their admirable characteristics of perfection and refinement.

The fact is that earlier stars were hired on the basis of their faces. Some had acting talent, but in many cases that was secondary to the face. Today, it is talent, but is it also the hair and body that rules. Cases in point: Jennifer Anniston and Sarah Jessica Parker—take away the hair and the bodies and just show the face.

Exceptions: My future star granddaughters.

Well, okay, for proof and discussion purposes compare your own groupings of countenance features of the then-and-now in the Hollywood community.

And while you're at it, don't you think that modern actress, Maggie Gyllenhaal has similarly-appealing features as did earlier actress, Claudette Colbert? (I met Claudette Colbert at one of Frank Sinatra's house parties. Elegant . . . simply an elegant lady.)

&

If the eyes of a person can reveal one's soul, I believe that one's voice and laughter can be just as revealing.

&

To the Washington, D. C. establishment:

ENOUGH!!!

Signed: The Messenger

&

I most certainly do believe in and support the moralistic principles of Christianity and Judaism.

Personally, I have strayed from those principles often during my life, none of which I am proud, but all of which I hope to atone.

That said, I cannot understand how a Muslim defends the Koran in its instructions to kill others and me on the basis that others and I are "infidels". That is an example of "religious teachings"?

&

I recently read a report on a scientific projection that it takes 500 years for a plastic bag to fully deteriorate. The columnist, Debra L. Saunders, of the Creators Syndicate, parenthetically questions "How does anyone know it takes 500 years for a bag to disintegrate?"

Well, Ms. Saunders, Bruce here: The answer is they don't specifically know. However, take a piece of plastic bag and put it in a dump field environment; check back within a certain length of time (a couple of years) to scientifically measure the extent of the deterioration of the sample piece; then multiply that measurement by mass of the entire plastic bag. There you have an equation from which one can then project an accurate answer to your question.

My question is: What becomes of the disintegration? Does it somehow metabolize or undergo a metamorphic transformation and just float off into space? If it becomes gaseous, is that not a subsequent by-product, if you will, of the deterioration process? Would the gases be absorbed by the atmosphere? Or not? In which case, where does it go? What *is* its transformation?

I would say that through the answer to the disintegration questions, and a related thorough study of earthly air, can we humans derive deeper insights in the past.

Which brings me to . . .

&

The Study of Air.

Questioning, for example, whether there are certain chemicals or elements not found in earthly particles presently existing in our air?

Of course there are; we've sustained meteors from space, haven't we?. Talking about spooky (there that Einstein word again). How about elements left in our atmosphere from our alleged interplanetary visitors? You know, the feared "aliens from another planet".

BTW: Looks like we might have to invent new space boogymen in view of us not finding any aliens on Mars—thus far that is; not to mean that they have been completely ruled out. I'd hope for visitors from Pluto on account of we could then call them Plutoniums.

If we have been visited, wouldn't there be traces of, let's say, particles of an exhaust system vehicle? Well, on second thought, I seriously doubt *that* on the basis that an exhaust is the result of what would be an old technology, but I use the example as a possible lead source of discovery.

Most certainly, alchemists have proved that there are many airs or "mystery gases" present on earth. Isn't it reasonable to expect that further scientific research would reveal un-earthly particles?

Isn't it therefore possible that such "new airs" would contain other clues to inter-planetary travel? After all, everything from hydrogen and phosphorous to laughing gases have only recently been discovered within the past century or two or three.

And we haven't touched the surfaces in understanding so-called Mystical, or Supreme systems. Nor have we fully examined certain philosophies such as Neoplatonism for clues in understanding numerous wonders of the universe, including many of those similarly-related mysteries here on Earth.

Frankly, I would prefer that, while we're here, Earth's mysteries be cleared-up before we squiggile around the Universe looking for clues.

As you know, we've known about atoms for less than a century and we're just getting into that void scientifically known as sub-atomic particles. All of which tells me that atomic discovery in only in its infancy.

Riding the space transfer rail of yet another new air, if you will?

Gases contain particles and electrons. So are electrons the drivers of my little squiggilies' theory? Is the creation of life therefore the smaller version of the Big Bang theory?

Years ago, a friend of mine from the Nevada Test Site responded to my question of how large is the Universe by saying that the important question is, how small?

&

The New Revised Version of the English Language: Drop the verbs.

It isn't your's; it is yo. It isn't they are or they're; it is just, they.

"They ain't yo goats, they be mine."

Etc., etc.

We be speaking Ebonics before long. Won't happen? Pointing out that there are very few world languages that *haven't* been injected by broader and diverse societies, cultures and languages.

Personally, I would prefer that we all speak decent English.

&

Darling—What a perfectly formed and defining word.

&

I think that a sensible new business operating model for the United States Post Office (USPO) would be to scale itself down and narrow its services exclusively confined to letters, printed advertisements and maintain its small flat-rate package services only.

Leave the package stuff to the other guys. Think of mail being mail, not freight.

Niche marketing sometimes makes better sense.

&

There are two types of laws in my country. There is man's law, which in some cases ensures order, and there is God's law.

Sometimes we confuse one with the other.

We Americans have a Constitutional (man's law) right to bear arms. After all, man has carried weapons of some sort for eternity. Spears have always been man's constant companions (God's survival law).

This gun issue is discussed elsewhere in this little book.

&

I suppose that the development of the ego helps to counter-balance the self-realization of one's shortcomings, aka/insecurities.

And despite the disagreements within certain accepted terms and definitions, the ego is the driver of all success.

It has to be in you. Some call it pride. Does ego drive pride? Vice versa?

Egos and women are often the drivers for men to engage in activities to acquire power.

And power and money are often what drive most women to select certain men.

&

And isn't having a white woman in hand the new status symbol for black men?

And will those particular women deny that size matters?

&

When you were a kid did you use your bed sheets to make tents?

And when you were a male kid, did you make, albeit smaller ;>) tents?

And if you are now a man, do you still make those little tents?

I did and do . . . fun isn't it?

Come on guys . . . 'fess up.

&

Ours is an economy basically predicated on "growth".

If the economy does not grow, i.e., get bigger and bigger, economists and investors refer to the economy as declining, or "shrinking" or being "stagnant", or "depressed" or "receding", as in titling "The Great Depression" or "The Great Recession".

Unfortunately, most of our utility needs, such as electricity, are based on a growth principle that is beholden to company shareholders. I think that utilities ought to be nationalized in America so as to stabilize and predict the costs of such necessary-to-life commodities

Where I live in Nevada, it seems that every few months the utilities' companies are going before a politically stacked power commission board pleading for more and more rate increases with their sob stories. They use the familiar negotiating tricks of asking for more and receiving perceived less, but always more than they really wanted in the first place. (I call it the deceptive psychological staging of price points. It's a combination twist on the ninety-nine cent theory and the drawing-back-of-prices' theory. For example, in gasoline pricing, prices are systematically raised almost daily on any excuse until there is a consumer outcry, at which point the oil companies then begin the process of rolling back the prices. But . . . . the damage is already done. The rollback only reaches back to a level that establishes a new high from whatever the product was prior to the systematic price increase. Three steps forward; one step back; three cents forward . . . just like the gasoline pricing scheme—with a point-ninety-nine cent or percentage element factored in.) "No madam, this product does not cost fifty dollars; it only costs forty nine dollars and ninety nine cents." "So in your mind, Madam, you only paid forty dollars for that lamp", so smirks the clerk.

Same thing with that "originally-priced" sales' deception. And how about that: "But wait! Order now and receive one free!!!" b.s.

The system dictates that the *poor* utility companies ostensibly have to pay the stockholder piper; in reality, it is us captive consumers who are the ones who have to satisfy the company piper.

I am sick of utility rate hearings. They are so damn rigged.

I attended a Utilities Commission hearing during which I asked the board to whom the electric company was beholden. The answer from one of the board members was that the electric company was beholden to its customers. "Wrong", I said, "the electric company is beholden to its stockholders".

Here's how that tune goes: Stockholders (investors) invest in utility companies for the specific purpose of receiving both increased value of their stock holdings and to receive periodic dividends as a result of (in this case, electric) companies' financial results. Those results are predicated on that previously pointed out factor of growth; growth is determined by profit; in order to achieve the most profitability from a business entity basically requires that revenues be periodically enhanced through what is referred to as price points, the rule of which is then therefore applied, which in turn affects another working principle, the never-ending cycle that is best described in one word: inflation.

One easy-to-understand example is that when gas prices go up, everything goes up. It costs the trucker more; it costs the consumer more; yet, interestingly it does not negatively affect the utility company's profitability. They simply go before those rigged utility commissions and "request" rate increases which are passed solely on to the consumer.

Gotta' satisfy the investors. To hell with the rate-paying consumers.

It can therefore be successfully argued that utility companies' satisfy stockholders' thirst for both profits and stock value through constant price increases that are passed to the hapless captive consumer. Granted that there are repair, improvement and expansion of services' factors formulated in utility companies' costs that can only be matched or covered through rate increases. However, we can agree, can't we, that constant price increases of utilities are the foundation basis for inflationary increases, and that inflation itself is the killer of any national economy. Pre-Hitler Germany is a good example of the subsequent effects and harm of a nation caused by that dreaded monetary dragon, inflation.

In the above paragraph, I use the adjective, constant, accurately. Otherwise, why would there even be a utilities commission which is constantly summoned to convene regarding utility rate increases rather regularly? And have you any knowledge of utility commissions' flat-out total denial of rate increases "requested" by the utility companies?

And while I am on the subject, why do water districts, such as in Nevada, need completely unnecessary and wasteful advertising budgets or fund support programs? Provide me with clean water.

I am of the political persuasion that believes in assembling the best parts of proven economic models and molding them into one cohesive and comprehensive financial and economic system. Certainly, one way of restraining the devastating effects of inflation is for American consumers and businesses to be provided a steady flow of their energy needs through an efficiently delivered product at a dependably affordable price point.

I could probably write an entire thesis on the economic stages that are directly affected by utilities' costs alone to the American consumer. One aspect of the theory is that, in general, consumers rarely and barely catch up with utility rate increases, particularly through their own comparable individual salary increases, before the next rate increase(s) take(s) effect. Thus is the day-by-day, week-by-week, month-by-month financial struggle battled constantly by most Americans.

The strategic economics of power company rate increases are explained through the same rhyme and song version of the "Bone Song" theory. Follow the bouncing ball and sing along:

The share holder demands dividends and growth in the value of their stock holdings; that demand is predicated on the simple principle of profit; in order to increase profits and stock values, the energy companies are continuously forced to increase the cost of its products and services.

It is an ever-increasing cycle. That is why I advocate for the establishment of American non-profit utility companies. They don't have to be government-run; they just have to not depend on profit or stock investment motives in providing Americans with dependable, efficient and affordable utility power needs.

Seniors and low-income households would benefit.

There would also be a positive windfall effect against inflation.

But I digress . . .

Not all successful (keyword here: successful) economies are based on growth. In fact, there are several global economies that do not depend on getting bigger and bigger or requiring more and more incremental increases. These are the local economies that do not require more and more profitability in order to satisfy investors. So-called economic stagnancy and realistic expectations of dependability are important factors that are just fine for millions of people globally.

As long as these local economies throughout the world provide basic needs, such as food, shelter, clothing, clean water, and a decent crop comes in, and a cow, goat or donkey has a calf or kid, those are the factors in defining a healthy, non-stressful economy sans a growth requirement. It is more of a continuation economic model.

Frankly, those are the most important elements in the life of most Afghans, and they like it that way.

"Yes, of course, Mr. President", the presidential advisors have wrongly and stupidly advised, "The people of Afghanistan want to emulate the American Way of Life."

No they don't, say I, they like their mountain caves and villages and mountain goats, thank you very much.

You get the picture.

And if you are among those who just don't understand, and as I have screaming for years: WE NEED TO GET THE HELL OUT OF THERE NOW!!!

&

Entitlements:

First of all, Social Security is not an "entitlement", as defined in today's sickening political lexicon. Nor are Social Security and Medicare recipients on the government dole, excepting the illegal immigrant with the fake Social Security card.

Americans <u>earned</u> it. They legitimately worked their asses off and paid into the (forced) system sometimes for years, sometimes for decades.

The system known as Social Security is a personal investment system that was enacted by President Franklin D. Roosevelt and administered and enforced by what has become a truly massive agency of the United States government.

Have you ever seen the extraordinary size of the Social Security office complex in Baltimore? Have you even factored in the astounding costs of local Social Security offices at every corner in America? The operations, payroll and employee retirement costs alone gobble up the revenue input. Have you any idea of the operating costs for the Social Security system?

Those of us who are in the system have paid into the system for every working year of our lives.

But the Social Security system is not a government "entitlement" as it is described and lumped in today's sickening political groupings. It is a definitive Ponzi Scheme, but paradoxically it isn't a Ponze Scheme (clearly defined separately as two entirely different systems, one legal, one illegal, by the spelling of what Ponzi and Ponze systems are—thank you very much, Mr. Clinton, for your "is" assistance in defining and therefore delineating the two entirely different systems. The Social Security System, you know, the one that is *not* a Ponzi scheme, is a working person's retirement investment system. An investment, by the way, that is not at all guaranteed or even prudent relative to its investment return (ROI). Nor does the Social Security money belong to anyone or anything related to government. Okay, so then why is it that we Americans are not marching on and jailing the thieves of our trusted government investment program, and garnishing the wages and assets of the criminals with the same compassion for them as they had for us while stealing our retirement funds?

Wall St. protesters: Are you listening?

&

To understand the current American government mentality requires the acknowledgment that there has to be employment created by government to employ much of an otherwise un-educated, un-trained and un-employable mass of humanity in this country.

But does it have to be on a cradle-to-grave basis, Mr. President and Mr. and Ms. Congresspersons?

And doesn't my 1998/2002 Channeling Plan for Education make better sense?

Wouldn't many of those government (office) workers prefer to be out working at a profession that they love, enjoy, and are very good at?

The Channeling Plan for Education.—Bruce Westcott circa1998/2002

&

Is it we or the system that is failing our children, or is it parents who are failing our children?

Oh come on now, everyone knows the truthful answer to that question.

Get your head out of the sand, aka/out of your ass, and realize and admit that it's the students who are failing in school.

Just listen to them talk . . .

I have seen no historical adaptation of young Abraham Lincoln studying by the fireplace with having his parents leering over his shoulder.

And the longer that we accept and perpetuate any of the damn excuses for the school failures, the worse we, as a nation, will become.

Do YOU Want The Truth?

&

While on the subject of us being God's children, please consider the following *generalities*:

- Blacks are superior athletes.
- Jews and the Irish have superior business acumen.
- Europeans are the best artists, artisans and builders.
- Italians are the best cooks.

- The English, Russians and Germans are the smartest scientists.
- The Chinese are the best mathematicians.
- Japanese people are the best innovators and most polite race of people on Earth.
- Greeks and Italians are the finest sculptors.
- Indians of both dominant sectarians and Muslims all over the world are the most sacred of peoples.
- China will obviously become the most dominant of all nations—if it hasn't already. However, excepting insuring and protecting their mineral and commodities' interests, I see China as having neither interest nor appetite for a geographical expansionistic role in the rest of the world. Not only does China have enough population on its plate to contend with and manage; they simply have neither real interest nor affinity for other peoples of the world. China looks after China. There should be a lesson there for America in that the United States ought to heed the Chinese model and take care of America.
- Russians are the best novelists and musical composers in the world. (Somewhat conversely, perhaps the most ruthless of peoples as well.)
- The Irish are the best poets.
- Italians are the best singers. (And its men are generally considered the most handsome.)
- Scandinavian women are the fairest of them all.
- Spanish and Italian women are the most beautiful and voluptuous. Persian women are the most intriguingly beautiful. Porto Rican and Brazilian women are the most excitingly appealing. Oh, those Hungarian women. English women are the most intelligent. And Italian women are the best cooks.
- The Greeks were the best philosophers upon which all insightful philosophy is predicated.

151

- The French are the most romantic.
- The English, Germans, Italians and Greeks are the best orators. It's a toss-up.
- The Italians and Greeks were, but now the Chinese are the best architects.
- Medical research and health care is best in America.
- Modern technology and scientific breakthroughs and discoveries come from America, China, Germany, and Japan.
- The Portuguese are the best fishermen.
- The Vikings were the best circumnavigators.
- The Dutch are the quaintest people of Earth.
- The Slavs are the toughest.
- The Arabs, Persians and Mongolians, in consideration of their barren landscapes and conditions, are the most resourceful people on Earth.
- The people of India and Pakistani regions have the highest untapped and unleashed brainpower potential.
- Same to same of the peoples of Southeast Asia, particularly the Southern Asians and an imminently, therefore easily projected, united Korea.
- It is relatively too early in the establishment of Australia and New Zealand to determine their historical greatness status. However it is a fact worth noting that the vast majority of inhabitants of those regions of the world are of English and Celtic descent boding well in terms of projected greatness. Also it seems that the "Down Under" continent and surrounding regions have the best chance for surviving the imminent nuclear holocaust.

Author's note:

My heart and sorrow, as does some of my genealogy (Cherokee), dwell with the American Indians. But the good news is that if they and other original dwellers on this earth can survive the imminent nuclear war(s), they can emerge and over time restore this planet to its original beauty. I hope so.

&

Shock and horror:

My presumption is that at that exact moment of our ultimate demise, we are shocked by death. Look at death masks: Do you see any smiling going on?

(Well, with the possible exception of Nelson Rockefeller . . . Now there was a guy who lived the fullest of life and allegedly died at the climax of a sexual encounter with a beautiful woman. Man what a way to come and go, so to speak . . . I, for some reason, think of what would have happened to Nelson Rockefeller after he died.)

Then, and Nelson Rockefeller aside, what happens afterwards reveals the truth of all religions, doesn't it?

&

Question: What is the common denominator that is prevalent as being the main cause of destitution of our once-great cities in the United States of America?

Look at the reality of slums and crime in Camden, Newark, Atlanta, Baltimore, Washington, D.C., Tupelo, New Orleans, Miami, Oakland, Detroit, and specific sections of otherwise great cities, such as the South Central and Watts' sections of Los Angeles, Dallas, Houston, Philadelphia, Atlantic city, Cleveland, St. Louis, and the squalor in countries such as

Haiti and Cuba, and much of the Caribbean and most of Africa.

Look at it realistically and honestly.

You must admit, if only to yourself, that there is a specific common denominator that is prevalent in those blighted areas of the United States and that is emulated throughout Africa (actually it is vice-versa), which is: It is the people, the inhabitants of the cities. And do you want the truth? It is mostly the black people inhabitants of those cities.

There's a 99% factor for you.

Call me what you will. My reply will be same as always, which is that we must begin to face, understand and admit the situation in order to solve the situation.

&

Come on black people: You CAN do better. I believe it!

Do YOU Want The Truth?

&

I learned that in the face of danger and imminent harm, it is always reassuring to be armed.

At least in most cases, you have a 50/50 chance of survival.

God bless the 2nd Amendment, despite its obvious ambiguity (again, why does the 2nd Amendment require interpretation?)

Re-write it.

&

Just a little more on the subject of the 2nd Amendment:

I think that the 2nd Amendment, which clearly states the government's approval of the "right" for a citizen to "bear arms" in the defense of one's country, life, property, pursuit of happiness, and against government tyranny is rather moot.

Government is, always has been and always will be superseded by any and all moral rights and obligations granted and demanded by our Creator.

And even if you don't believe in the Creator, you nevertheless have a right and/or a moral obligation to defend yourself in the face of impending harm. Under such circumstance, it would then be your choice to either accept the Biblical concept of a turned cheek, or not.

If we rightfully insist on having a 2nd Amendment to the Constitution of the United States, it ought to, as noted above, be stated in such a way as to not require its "interpretation" by a majority vote of a panel or committee consisting of nine people.

Yes, the 2nd Amendment is clear to me, but not at all clear to the police, nor the courts in this country.

Re-write the 2nd Amendment. Clear it all up once and forever.

That's my position on the issue. What's yours?

&

I do sometimes wonder if God is <u>not</u> the physical Creator of the Universe. I wonder because I honestly do not know.

(Let's see if celebrated atheists, Christopher Higgens or Madeline Murry can come back from the dead and tell us.)

Rather, is it that God exists and rules, directs, and instructs and allows destiny or happenstance to occur confined to and within Her own spiritual realm and not concern Herself with the physical realm of us trashy little humans?

Is it that God resides and rules, if you will, throughout in the far more powerful spiritual dimension that exists within the weaker, therefore vulnerable physical nature aspect of the Universe?

If God does reside in all Earthly humanity and nature (the Buddhist theory), why not then throughout the entire Universe? And why does God not concern Herself exclusively with the physicality of all things in the Universe?

We humans justify the concept of such things as merely being "physical"; sex being the most prevalent of such (lame) explanations.

"Oh, it's just a physical thing". Sure lady . . .

There is nothing emotional or spiritual? Just physical? Just mental? I say that it's both, and more.

Perhaps God is not all that concerned with any of the physical dimensions and experiences, having quite enough of a challenge—yes, I assume that God has challenges—with other dimensions that we humans have yet to discover.

&

If you listen to him, don't you agree that Rush Limbaugh sounds more and more like William F. Buckley?

Stretch those vowels, Rush.

&

Rush: Vat, r u klazzy?

Of course there's global warming.

Geeeeze . . .

&

Let us read the Pledge of Allegiance: ". . . to the flag of the United States of America and to the Republic for which it stands".

The national pledge to our country and to our flag stands for the *Republic*, not the/a democracy.

And whatever happened to "One nation under God, indivisible, and with liberty and justice for all"? Where did that go since the recent onslaught of political correctness?

The United States of America is *not* divided? We citizens cannot mention God in our public expressions and our national mottos? Get your head out of the sand, my fellow Americans. Become patriotic. Rise and be proud to be an American.

Yes, I know, it is difficult to do in consideration of the twisted sickness and brainwashing campaign by much of the influential media.

YOU ARE BEING BRAINWASHED, STUPID!

Truth is that this is yet another reason to not appreciate the forced and politically expedient diversity of this nation.

Forced diversity is no longer necessary. Ask Oprah.

But some of it is still perpetuated. They're bitching now about the Academy Awards committee as being not diverse enough. The Color Purple, The Help, Driving Ms. Daisy, Wings, and practically all of the current television shows notwithstanding, as if talent can only be recognized and acknowledged through a more "diverse" (read: racial) committee of peers?

&

The pageantry recently showcased to the premier of China was less about solidifying substantial and meaningful United States' relations, business and numerous aspects of cooperation between us and China as much as it was for Barrack and Michele Obama to bask in the international spotlight.

Why else did we revel in such ridiculously expensive and unnecessary nonsense? Give me one good reason.

If I have to buy a friendship . . . .

Well, you get that picture too.

Important to note that on November 16, 2011, mere months following the ridiculously expensive pageantry afforded to the Chinese president, Mr. Obama was in Australia pissing off that very same Chinese representative.

&

And while we're on the subject of out-of-control government spending, as I have previously stated for a very long period of time, I advocate for sending <u>nothing</u> in the way of dollar bills to Israel and Egypt from the coffers and on the backs of the American Taxpayers.

All welfare reform, both personal and corporate, is not just needed; it is imperatively necessary to the future of our nation and our children.

The truth be told: Why is it that the American Taxpayer is "responsible" for any international welfare that is disingenuously passed on to us in the name of Foreign Policy?

The answer: We aren't, and if I have anything to do with it, we are simply not going to give our hard-earned dollars to one and all international ingrates. And, least of all issues relative to this matter, it is a fact that the Foreign Aid policies of our nation are at the core root unconstitutional.

Ask Davey Crockett.

Aren't there 10 billionaires or enough millionaires of both Arab and Jewish persuasions to accept the responsibility of aiding Israel and Egypt?

Can you get that concept, Mr. Government? How about understanding and accepting the fact that taxpayer money isn't your money to spend on unconstitutional issues, matters and foreign nations, particularly corrupt foreign nations. Can you spell Iraq, Afghanistan, Pakistan, Karzai, Maliki?

Can you understand that? Because if you cannot understand such an easy-to-comprehend explanation, you need to step aside . . . now.

Yes, Mr. Government, it is true that the runaway overdraft of the American Taxpayer's account is unconstitutional. However, and as proved recently, you ignore budgeting, which is a fundamental thing, and as Coach Vince Lombardi preached, it's the fundamentals, stupid.

Let's get some sensibility injected into our failed Foreign Policies.

And while we're at it, and I repeat: I say we get the hell out of the entire Middle East.

Upon our full withdrawal of physical presence from the Middle East, we can remind the world that Israel is our ally. And as such, there ought not to be any question or misunderstanding that the United States of America shall vigorously and conclusively defend and help protect all of our international allied commitments.

We're just no longer going to send them money.

&

Plant life intelligence:

It makes sense to my understanding that plants possess some sort of "brain" sensibility or sensitivity-driven internal mechanism.

For example, this morning I added a string to a trellis for one of my climbing vines to attach to and follow my designated path above the entrance to my front door.

Within minutes, the vine had sensed the string and had clung to and had already begun to make its upward climb. (Of course wind had something to do with it, but the vines depend on that travel source of nature.)

The same sort of plant intelligence or sensibility or sensitivity is inherently inbred in humans and animals. This inherent instinct example testifies to what you and I and most other humans and animals experience when rock or mountain or climbing. (In that regard, and as an avid rock climber myself, wouldn't it be cool in musing to have a beanstalk stairway to the Heavens, such as in the mythical Jack and The Beanstalk?)

Doesn't this sort of sensibility require some sort of activation in plants? A "brain" perhaps?

Or do we simply pass it off or categorically cast it, as I did above, as being "nature at work". If that is so, then it is clear to me that nature itself obviously has its own sets of sensibilities and intelligence that is intentionally applied selectively.

Or am I somewhat contributing to the selective process theory?

Let's take a shower.

Most humans of other languages have an understandable difficulty in the understanding itself of such English/American phrases such as, let's take a shower, or I took a shower; I am going to take a pee, or I took a pee; or we took a vacation, etc.

The replies to such examples of phrases above can be equally confusing to students who were studying English. For instance, "Yes, thank you, I think that I shall accept your suggestion and take a pee."??? . . . Very puzzling to others.

I briefly studied Japanese at the Tohoku University in Sendai, Japan, where I was asked by one of the teachers as to whether or not I thought that Japanese was a difficult language to learn. My immediate response was to tell the teacher that yes, the Japanese language is difficult to master considering that the language is expressed in four different written forms, primarily Hiragana, Katakana, and Kanji characters, and includes a modern form of writing English words and phrases called Romanization.

However, I continued with the teacher, I was very glad I wasn't trying to learn Basic English that is written and spoken in so many dozens of various forms, dialects, accents and constantly newly-coined words and phrases that it, as my southern grandparents would say, makes your head swim.

&

"Whatever will be will be." (Oh, help me, please, what is the Spanish interpretation? Kasara sara . . . . or something similar to it.)

Argue and dissect, if you will, the above statement relative to its philosophy, pertinence and explanation.

Is it true that there is a destiny factor involved in such a phrase of resignation, some of which is touched on in this publication, or can we alter what will be through actions of our own making and efforts?

I believe that all of the split-second decisions that we make daily take us on very specifically different paths.

Whatever . . .

&

Just for the conversation: In Earthly physics, gravity is what makes things fall down, right, Sir Newton? In Universal physics, doesn't gravitational pull prevent things from traveling upwards as well?

Whatever . . .

&

I and all men want room to roam naturally and privately in my home.

&

A man's home is his castle.

&

Copied from an e-mail exchange with a close friend:

My friend writes:

"Bruce, during the Nazi siege of Leningrad during World War II, Russian scientists literally starved rather than eat the seeds of one of the most important living collections of plant materials on Earth. The building that has housed the collection for decades and its entire contents is now in danger of being bulldozed in favor of building condos."

My reply:

"Don, this is a shameful development from many aspects, but just as humans have contaminated our water supplies, the willful destruction of the foundations of the staff of life, food, is no surprise.

Sometimes, Don, I think that maybe the sooner we humans destroy ourselves the better for not only Mother Earth, but other planets and galaxies throughout the Universe as well.

Perhaps madness is the most serious of human defects. Up until recently, humans have only been bent of destroying each other at a maddening pace. Now, with the advent of the Industrial Age, it is the very planet in and on which humans exist that is headed for annihilation. If that doesn't define stupidity and madness . . ."—Bruce

&

A message from this taxpayer to all government employees:

Excuse me Madam and Sir, but you work for me.

&

Money Is worthless . . . if not eventually spent.

Getting back to the National Sales Tax and my previous question regarding the taxation of drugs that I wanted you to ponder:

What would the taxation received by our government amount to if every aspect of the entire drug trade were to be taxed? I can tell you most assuredly that you and I will pay less taxation and therefore able to spend substantially more of our own money on our own choices.

Same question regarding every bit of theft and crime committed over the issue of money, including every bit of underground commerce, including criminal and every cent of under-the-table exchanges of money: How much additional taxation revenues would you say would be received by our government?

Well, get this:

It is only at the point of sales of products or exchange of services that the fairest, most equitable and sensible system of taxation kicks in, which is the implementation of a National Sales Tax.

Eliminate the Income Tax and its overseer, the XVI Amendment.

Corporate taxation would be revised as well if I were the President.

With having a Sales Tax structure, grocery items such as food would be exempt. All services, including the providing of legal, accounting and financial services would be taxed.

All underground commerce, estimated in terms of $trillions, including another $trillion drug trafficking commerce would be subjected to taxation. All other products would be taxed based on an assessment of need and desirability for the products on a sliding scale basis. The Department of Commerce can easily provide assessors with all of the data and assorted other information necessary to categorize and apply these taxation tables.

Again, unspent money is worthless, but would be subjected to an equal and equitable taxation assessment only at the point of sales and the providing of services.

The Flat Tax idea is no good on account of it depends on exactly the same criteria of honest and truthful reporting and filings to the IRS that exists today. And we know what that truth is.

And the exact same principles depend on all persons doing any kind of business in America to file an honest reporting of their incomes, and we all know that ain't gonna' happen either.

With the establishment of a Sales Tax, everyone who spends the money, whether earned, stolen, or regardless of however or from wherever the money is derived, is taxed equally.

Each of us can invest in everything and anything that is recommended, advised, or of our own personal choice. We will not be taxed at the source of our successes and efforts, regardless of how it is derived, until the money is <u>spent</u>.

We would still need the IRS for collection enforcement and financial recording purposes, but there would not be a need for any additional printing costs for the establishment of any new agency's stationary, identification and purpose. It will still be the IRS. Collection duties of this agency of the Federal Government will be re-focused.

A National Sales Tax—The fairest and most equitable form of taxation, and it comes with a full collection guarantee. Imagine the staggering amount of taxation-derived revenues our government would receive from such a beautifully sensible plan. And if applied properly, there would be an enormous windfall benefit in addressing our national economic necessities, such as paying down our—which would be negotiated in my administration—national debt.

Fair, equitable, efficient, and sensible. And we and our international trading partners participating in equally fair trade policies and practices would be a whole lot better off if we were to completely trash the current tax code in the United States.

We'll personally receive every penny of our earned wages and investments. Taxation would occur only at the point of sales.

Our nation will still need the IRS as a collection and enforcement agency. (No need for an agency name change—too much stationary costs. ICE: Are you listening?)

We'll still need accountants.

We'll still need financial advisors.

We can make and keep as much money as we can.

We can stuff our mattresses with it; we can wallpaper our rooms with it; we can burn it in our fireplaces; we can save and invest it in any financial endeavor or matter of our choosing.

And we can spend it in any way of our choosing.

But the money is not taxed until it is spent.

Let me review: Every single cent of every single dollar, regardless or irrespective of how it is derived will be taxed.

That's right, everything from Wall St. bonuses to everything related to drugs, crime, or any other form of underground commerce.

It is the ultimate "Fair Share" tax structure.

A National Sales Tax: The solution to the major problems that burden us and completely eliminates our absurdly and unnecessarily-complex taxation structure and code.

&

As great an orator and national leader, and because of his stupidity as a military strategist as was Adolph Hitler, I blame him for preventing Germany from becoming the greatest nation on Earth. God what a waste of human potential!

Hitler is fully responsible for the annihilation of an impossibly undetermined amount of brilliant brainpower, productivity and talent within his own citizenry.

The cost to the world and including, but not excluding others, the loss of 6 million Jews during that shameful period in history is equally as tragic and immeasurable.

And yet, the survivors and what they have built from the ashes of one of history's most wasteful excursions in warfare is a testament to the courage, resolve and resilience of Eastern and Western Europeans and Jews everywhere in world.

No finer testament necessary.

Think of the American and the British, and the French and the Italian, the Poles, Russians and other nations' contributions lost to the world in senseless battles.

That damn stupid Hitler.

And I cannot imagine the devastating setbacks that Japan experienced through their stupidity in engaging in warfare by awakening the "Sleeping Tiger". As sensible and resourceful as they have ultimately proven themselves otherwise both before and since the war, what in the Hell were they thinking? Admiral Yamamoto was right. Japan awakened a sleeping giant, the United States of America.

If I were an Iranian, I would ask that the Iranian leadership consider ending its annihilation-baiting rhetoric before they are the ones annihilated. Iranians are wonderful people and Iran is an incredibly beautiful and historically-interesting country that I would love to visit; it's the leadership . . .

Repeating: Japan has actually achieved all of their pre-WWII objectives not militarily, but economically.

Count me among those who advocate for an end of war. However, please be reminded also I have no compunction to pull the trigger in defense of my family and loved ones, my life, and my nation.

&

I believe in the economic sense of having a 4%-6% or a 3%-5% range of financial interest investment and borrowing standards.

Three to four percent return encourages savings, and 5-6% is a reasonable average rate of return (ROI) on investments.

Current zero percentage interest rates are unproductive simply on the basis that they yield and therefore produce nothing. So, where's the real incentive?

Based on that premise, I advocate for re-establishing interest rate standards.

Maybe that would re-invigorate our economy. And, perhaps as well, the Fed (which I would prefer to not exist) has erred on the wrong side of setting interest rates.

Has there been a correlation with lower interest rates and a worsening economy?

Just something for economists to consider . . . .

&

One thing about our government shutdowns, whether real or threatened, is that (have you noticed?) somehow the bureaucracies always manage to keep their taxation accruing, bills flowing, and collections enforced.

While I continue to be in an appreciative and congratulatory mood, I think that it is time for the world to recognize and credit the incredibly important and meaningful contributions made to mankind everywhere by white people.

&

Birds

. . . are considered by many as adorable. The reality is that birds are violent and viciously nasty little creatures.

Birds are the definitive example of physical deception. They are a pre-historic species that had existed prior to, and have survived through, an otherwise unexplainable event or set of events such as the occurrence of the extinction of most, but not all, of the animals of the Jurassic period.

(In fact, it would interesting for scientists to note that birds and insects survived, but animals on the ground perished during the Jurassic holocaust. So, if that were the case, how would it be explained how and why winged dinosaurs perished with their ground-dwelling brethren? There could be a clue, however, on the basis of this question for paleontologists to pursue.)

&

Oh, Monica Lewinsky, pray tell how it all happened

You weren't sexually aggressive were you? You know, like in the exchange of flashing eyes towards Bill's crotch?

My Dear: Of course you were.

Speaking of flashing, did you, Ms. Lewinsky? Is that how it all got started?

Did you ask Mr. Clinton to show and tell, thereby conclusively solving and settling the (in)famous riddle of Clinton's boxers or briefs?

And as you fondled Mr. Clinton's manhood while you buckled-up your presidential kneepads, did you and the President discuss foreign policy?

Not that there was anything new in the way of historical White House dalliances . . . but rather, in that the subject is now openly discussed.

&

Why is it that most women in business introduce themselves solely on a first-name basis while businessmen usually use both names?

&

Single Moms

Where are the fathers?

Oh, that's right, I forgot, government, i.e., taxpayers are responsible for the abandoned bastards of irresponsible males.

I am sympathetic, but clearly not responsible for these tender lives.

My dear mother raised three boys and supported my grandmother working as a "barmaid". And she proudly proclaimed that she "never took a dime of welfare".

Too often the "responsibility" of government sponsorship carries over to adulthood and passed through the filtration of the American Criminal Justice System.

However, don't blame it all on the males. I have overheard conversations between young women who advised their counterparts to have as many babies as possible in order to receive the most in government benefits.

Lay around on a couch, eat bon-bons, and pop out mo' babies, collect checks, the American Taxpayer be damned.

&

Interesting that Michelle Obama's June, 2011 trip to South Africa, and including Secretary Clinton's recent visit with Nelson Mandela, were both clearly and absolutely focused on South African blacks. There was no mention of the blatantly unadulterated racism and murderous ethnic cleansing towards white South Africans, the Campbell family in South Africa for example.

Why is that, Mrs. Obama and Mrs. Clinton? Why did you ignore the reverse-racism and conveniently overlook the carnage carried out by black Africans against South African white people?

Ask Neil Boortz about Rhodesia.

&

The Constitution is not what made this country great. The American People made this country great.

As a whole and as pointed out in this tome, the Amendments to the Constitution of the United States prevent the original Constitution from being a clearly defined document. If it were, and again as previously stated, we would not need interpretations based on the opinions of our Supreme Court, particularly of its Amendments. (Have you noticed that most of the Supreme Court dockets consist of questions and challenges specifically to our Constitutional Amendments?)

The Supreme Court usually hands down "opinions" on a Constitutional challenge based on a split majority. Worse, some Supreme Court decisions are undeniably based on a Justice's political bent, or social or cultural beliefs.

The very nature of appointments to the Supreme Court is political. Political presidents of the United States appoint Supreme Court Justices, who are then confirmed or rejected by the politically laden Congress of the United States.

Politics, politics, politics.

Whether the issues are religious, social, or political, the Supreme Court of the United States (SCOTUS) decisions are based on each and every one of the Justices' individual opinions, interpretations and political positions on issues.

Those are exactly among the factors that I would <u>not</u> want in having my legal matters decided.

Again, if laws were written clearly in the first place, we would not need an "opinion" of the law.

&

Murder/Suicide:

There is a fable about a scorpion that comes upon a monkey sitting on the shore of a riverbank preparing to cross the river.

The scorpion asks the monkey for a lift across the river, to which the monkey says to the scorpion, "But if I take you across the river, you are going to bite me and we'll both drown."

"No I won't", say the scorpion and eventually convinces the monkey to assist him across the river.

When the monkey, with the scorpion on his back, reaches about half-way across the river, sure enough, the scorpion reaches down and bites the monkey on the neck.

"That was stupid", says the monkey to the scorpion. "Why did you bite me? Now we're both going to die." The scorpion replies, "Sorry, Mr. Monkey, but I cannot resist my nature of being a scorpion."

The lesson analogy extension of the story is that Mr. Cancer somehow gets into Mr. Bloodstream, who. similarly to the monkey, says to Mr. Cancer, "But if you succeed in your mission to kill me, we're both going to die."

Well . . . you know the rest.

Nature's murder/suicide.

Does anything in life make any sense?

&

Is Socialism the scorpion on Capitalism's back?

&

In view of my somewhat bad boy reputation, some of you might find it surprising that two former Maryland governors had appointed me a Committing Magistrate (essentially a substitute judge).

One was a Democrat, Marvin Mandel (I was especially fond of the Mandel family members, including the Kovans, Polack, Swartz, Stofberg, Yerman, Goldstein and many related other Baltimore families); and the other was a Republican, Spiro Agnew, who became Richard Nixon's Vice President of the United States. Both of whom were disgraced while in public office. And one of whom (Mr. Mandel) was jailed.

Rod Blagojevich, you are not the first, nor will you be the last to feel the wrath of the American taxpayer for your despicable corruption while in trusted public office.

&

Is there anything more beautiful than a fire in the hearth?

Or fire in the belly of determined men and women?

&

Even the coined word, Internet, is brilliant.

I can visualize the discussion: "What shall we call it?", the founding inventors might have asked. "Well, what is it?"

could have been one of the rhetorical questions brought up during the discussion. "It's an international network of communications' connections." was possibly the reply.

"Let's call it the Internet" would have been a natural conclusion to the conversation.

So direct and simple. So brilliant. And the network system itself is not too bad either.

But I do not trust my government in believing that the Internet is not, nor will not, be "messed" with in the future.

&

Entirely too often we hear recent immigrants to America as referring to "my country" during conversations.

Troubling to me is that they are not referring the United States of America; instead they are fondly speaking of their country of origin from which they emigrated.

This is an example of what disturbs American citizens when they simply request of new immigrants to assimilate in American language, culture and customs, and to become as one in America.

If that is too much for our new immigrants to respect, please let me remind our otherwise appreciated guests that the doors to the borders of the United States swing both ways.

American citizens are as proud and nationalistic as the next fellow. Why then is it that we Americans are required by the world to accept or even tolerate the massive illegal invasion into our country?

I've laid out a plan to solve the current illegal immigration issue. In 2002, the plan was featured on the front page of an Internet publication founded and edited by former Senator Howard Dean's classmate at Yale, Richard Green. The plan received an impressive nod of agreement from others.

Why can't we receive the simple courtesy of being asked by others to allow their entrance into our nation? And then to have them feast upon the unwilling corpse of the American taxpayer? As my old buddy, Don King, famously put it: "Only in America".

And by the way, there is a pathway to citizenship in this country. It's no Yellow Brick Road, that's for sure. But my ex-wife Fumi and our sons, Hiroki and Taiga, successfully traveled the arduous bureaucratic journey.

So why can't the illegals?

&

Hair

In most instances, hair is usually referred to as that patch of follicles on one's head (or, in my bald-headed case, the absence of such follicle growth).

Hair on a human head is different; noticeably different to a point where we are often described by the hair, or lack thereof, on our heads. The shape and style, and the color of our hair is part of the human description of one another. Other than the color of our facial skin and facial growth of hair, rarely do we describe the human face. Instead, we describe both others and ourselves within the frame of our hair.

Weird.

Having hair on other parts of the human body is a strange and interesting, and complex twist of the human exterior anatomy.

For example, for most of us humans, hair grows on our toes and in our nostrils and ears, above our eyes, on our legs, on and under our arms, and in our pubic and anal areas. For some, hair grows on our backs and faces and down our necks.

But seldom do we recognize that hair on those areas of our bodies grow only to what seemingly are pre-prescribed length, thickness and concentration in certain areas. In those areas of our bodies, hair doesn't, or at least doesn't noticeably, fall out. And when and if it does fall out, it regenerates itself.

Why, God, oh why couldn't you have given us a regenerative process for hair on our heads?

&

Speaking of great hair:

Have you guys noticed that there are quite a few truly beautiful and intriguing Indian and Pakistani women out there in America more than before?

Just asking . . .

&

About 40 years ago, as I was sitting on the seashore of Miami Beach while, as many of us do, pleasantly sifting the sand through my fingers. It then occurred to me that sand is a by-product of crushed shells and bones of creatures that had been roaming the seas for the past zillions or so years. In that respect, sand is a by-product of death.

Which leads me to proffering the following theory for some of you to contemplate:

I believe that the accumulative passing of all living things on Earth contribute to the cylindrical expansion of the Earth.

Let's test the theory. Let's take a current measurement of the Earth. Then take another incremental measurement, say, a brief hundred thousand or ten billion years from today, I believe that it only makes sense that we will have proven that the Earth's circumference has expanded.

Taking the theory further, I have no doubt that our earthy and atmospheric environment exists within the vacuum contents of a huge metaphoric pressure cooker. As does everything within a pressure cooker, whether it is potatoes, fowl, or molecules, there is some sort of a shifting or contracting process that takes place. (Others can explain the process in basic physics terms.) So how much longer before it all goes boom as do all bubble enclosures?

Could we then further expand upon a basic explanation for the constant changes of our seas, mountains and even our continents? Is it possible that these kind of dramatic changes come about mostly due to downward pressures from our atmospheric layers above the Earth instead of originating from the internal core of the Earth? Or both? Sure, physically the earth changes from within, but—again—are these changes also the result of downward atmospheric pressures?

If that were the case, one could reasonably presume that the Earth's atmosphere is also expanding in a relative fashion to its dirt. However, within such an assumption there would possibly be a counter-elasticity resistance effect (if you will) from the Universe which would, in turn, explain the constant and continual force that causes the Universe itself to expand. A worse-case scenario with respect to this theory would be that the Earth's atmosphere or the Universe itself would be stretched to its limits and eventually burst. The ultimate Bubble Theory.

Keep in mind that bubbles are subject to a physics principle of overextended expansion. And then they too burst.

Just saying . . .

Taken from my more expansive notes on the subject, the furtherance of this theory would postulate that if the Earth's atmosphere were in fact expanding, that there would a natural cause and effect assumption that all planets are influenced by each other's atmospheric conditions and expansion. Do we depend on a self-adjustment with each other in respect to all planetary bodies within the Universe?

Certainly, if only one of our Milky Way planets or sizeable moons was to explode due to any type of pressure, we're all cooked gooses.

And so, what is dirt? It is, as is sand, a compost accumulation of all things previously living—that constantly increases the measurement of the Earth if you are in agreement with my expansion theory.

All of this does prove to me that the Earth and all of the Universe is so old in terms of measurement in years, that we have no idea of the age factors involved in neither the beginnings or the subsequent universal rotations of the Universe.

Age is timeless? It is in terms of accurately calculating time measurement. Time measurement relative to the Universe is absolutely impossible to determine and therefore absolutely meaningless. Interesting for theoretical discussion, but absolutely moot and meaningless in attempting to correctly speculate or quantify.

And finally on this point, is it reasonable to assume that the Earth and other Heavenly bodies in our galaxy started out as marble size "planets"?

Seems to me that planets and solar systems are the result of some sort of an accumulation of blasted mass that eventually formed a shape through a constant rotating process for many zillions of years. Well, why then are all things universal round and not square, or oblong, for example? The roundness of all things universally is further proof that all things evolve.

Of course, the question would then become, prior to this or any other Big Bang theory, what did the Universe originally consist of? Was there a great big blank canvas of gases? Where did the gases come from? How were they formed or coagulated? What was God's intent?

It seems to me that planets and solar systems are the result of some sort of an accumulation of blasted mass that eventually formed a shape through a constant rotating process for many zillions of years.

Of course, the question would then become what did the Universe originally consist of? Was there a great big blank canvas of gases? Where did the gases come from? How were they formed or coagulated? What was God's intent?

From how far away do comets come? Why are planets stationary in orbit and comets seemingly floundering in the universe? Is it another size matters' explanation? What is the gravitational explanation for the physics' discrepancies? Do planets eventually become so bloated that they fall within the perfect set of orbital circumstances in which to settle? Where do comets end up? Are comets and planets merely on a constant and predictable timetable trajectory around the universe as scientists have claimed? If so, doesn't that indicate that the universe is stationary or within some sort of enclosure and does not in fact expand? Everything else in the universe is circular. Are we just witnessing a natural rotation everything in the universe? What is that other "debris" that we see throughout space? What materials and atmospheric gases, therefore elements and particles, does it consist of? And why is it even there if not to prove the Big Band theory?

Again, we'll have to talk to God for those answers.

I do hope that we eventually find out.

&

Right now I am heeding the astute advice of Sophia Vergara to move my energy forward and to love and rebuild life.

&

In order to solve any problem requires a frank analysis, understanding and acceptance of the roots(s) of the problem(s).

The roots of the problems that besiege the United States are:

- The true (and mostly unrealized) inequality of the U. S. Tax Code (see my Sales Tax proposal)
- Oil and the Middle East (I've got solutions)
- Government corruption and corporate influence in government (see: Stupid Supreme Court ruling on the First Amendment)
- Outright Marxism in America
- Racism in America—both sides
- Illegal Immigration in America (I've proffered sensible solutions)
- Lack of effective congressional and presidential leadership

And the true stupidity of it all is that it all can be solved. However solutions require leadership.

This is the national change of course and phrase of understanding that our nation now requires:

W-e-re a-ll A-m-e-r-i-c-a-n-s! W-e-re a-ll i-n A-m-e-r-i-c-a T-o-g-e-t-h-e-r!

&

If I were the President of the United States of America, I would instruct our Treasury Secretary to secure interest-bearing long-term investment bonds to participate in the construction to widen and deepen the Panama Canal* in order to accommodate the next generation of larger and technologically advanced ships of seas.

* A South American jobs' and manufacturing boom as the United States simultaneously constructs the Great American

Wall and America's needed rebuilding and infrastructure projects will affect our entire North and South American continents. Now that would be a stimulus that would also create and expand worldwide manufacturing, trade and overall international economies.

Let's get ready and set our sights for the future while we create jobs right now.

&

In closing, I paraphrase the Beatles: In the end, the love you take is equal to the love that you contribute to all of God's nature.

And I especially like and can relate to Billy Joel's great line, "I may be crazy, but I'm not the lunatic you're looking for".

&

I am certain that my brother, Dickie (Richard Paul Westcott), will be recognized as the greatest of all rare combination of author/illustrator persons in the literary and art worlds.

Picasso could not match my brother's literary imagination, and Shakespeare cannot match my brother's artistic abilities, but Dickie crosses over both artistic fine lines. Period.

&

And that my daughter, Linda, will someday influence the political world with her brilliance, smarts, sophistication, entrepreneurial and management experience and ability, kindness and beauty.

And you should see and speak to Linda's daughters . . .

&

And lastly:

I am God.
So are you said Jesus, said Dr. Wayne Dwyer.
I am I said, said Neil Diamond.
I am that I am, said God.
Therefore, I am said I.

The End and thanks for listening.

Bruce Westcott

Reminder: Soon you'll be able to listen to Bruce Westcott singing and playing on OverTheMoonrecording.com CDs and apps everywhere.

Hook up an advance order through brucewestcott.org